PRIMARY Art

6588RB

Dianne Sterrett

PRIMARY ART *(Book C)*

Published by R.I.C. Publications® 2007

Reprinted 2008

Copyright© Dianne Sterrett 2007

ISBN 978-1-74126-469-2

RIC–6588

Titles available in this series:
PRIMARY ART *(Book A)*
PRIMARY ART *(Book B)*
PRIMARY ART *(Book C)*
PRIMARY ART *(Book D)*
PRIMARY ART *(Book E)*
PRIMARY ART *(Book F)*
PRIMARY ART *(Book G)*

Distributed by

AUSTRALIA: **R.I.C. Publications®**
PO Box 332, Greenwood WA 6924

UK: **Prim-Ed Publishing**
PO Box 2840, Coventry CV6 5ZY

IRELAND: **Prim-Ed Publishing**
Bosheen, New Ross, Co. Wexford

Internet websites

In some cases, websites or specific URLs may be recommended. While these are checked and rechecked at the time of publication, the publisher has no control over any subsequent changes which may be made to webpages. It is *strongly* recommended that the class teacher checks *all* URLs before allowing students to access them.

Website: www.ricpublications.com   www.prim-ed.com

Email: mail@ricgroup.com.au   sales@prim-ed.com

PRIMARY ART
Book C

Foreword

Primary art is a series of seven books designed to provide teachers with a collection of skills, ideas and techniques to support current curriculum requirements in the visual arts learning areas.

Titles in this series include:

- *Primary art – Book A*
- *Primary art – Book B*
- *Primary art – Book C*
- *Primary art – Book D*
- *Primary art – Book E*
- *Primary art – Book F*
- *Primary art – Book G*

Contents

R.I.C. Publications/Prim-Ed Publishing

Teachers notes

From the teacher

The activities within *Primary art* Books A–G, will provide teachers with a series of multiskilled, visual arts lessons and activities for a whole range of topics, themes and special events.

Covering all primary year levels, the series equips the busy classroom teacher with a range of lessons from the 'quick and easy' to the more sophisticated carrier projects that work over three to four lessons.

Each art project is accompanied by easy to use reflection and assessment record sheets, enabling the collection of relevant evidence to record student progress.

The reflection sheets provide a thoughtful evaluation of the student's own performance for each facet of the lesson.

Task assessment sheets provide a quick means to identify and record a student's performance in criteria which assess the given outcomes.

Within the series, students are given the opportunity to dabble with different media and to experience and build on a broad spectrum of techniques and skills, creating effects that will enhance their artistic work.

As the students build on their repertoire of skills, ideas and arts knowledge, they begin to plan and create a desired look or effect through experimentation. It is important to understand that the finished product will vary in quality according to the level of skill development.

As experience builds, so does the ability of students to use their artwork for purposes other than just the thrill of being creative. Their work becomes meaningful, with a purpose in society.

Dianne Sterrett

Art project activities

Art doesn't have to have high preparation requirements if basic supplies are kept well stocked. This can be achieved by enlisting an adult to collect and prepare materials.

Lessons throughout the series have been coded to identify the outcomes addressed or to indicate the effective use:

● **Arts ideas:** *Creates artworks to express ideas.*

● **Arts skills and processes:** *Uses a range of visual arts skills, techniques, procedures, practices and technologies.*

● **Arts responses:** *Uses an aesthetic understanding to acknowledge, reflect on and assess the arts.*

● **Arts in society:** *Demonstrates an understanding of the part that the arts play in society.*

★ *Enlist an adult to assist with the preparation of tasks, to help children in managing various tasks, or to mount work or add finishing touches to projects where adult skills are required.*

More able students may be able to complete for themselves activities designated as requiring parent or adult helpers. Mounting artworks is dependent on the availability of that resource. For that reason, this step—which relates to many of the artworks—is optional, except where required for support or where part of the artwork is displayed offset, for special effect.

Curriculum links

WA	VIC	NSW	QLD	SA
Arts ideas ●	Arts practice – Ideas, skills, techniques and process ● ●	Making ● ●	Visual arts – Making images and objects ● ●	Arts practice ● ●
Arts, skills and process ●	● ●		Visual arts – Making and displaying ● ●	Arts analysis and response ● ●
Arts responses ●	Responding to the arts – Criticism, aesthetics and contexts	Appreciating ● ●	Visual arts – Appraising images and objects ● ●	Art in context ● ●
Arts in society ●	● ●			

R.I.C. Publications/Prim-Ed Publishing

Teachers notes

Making life easy!

Setting up

Setting up a good resource base is essential for an effective art program, as having appropriate tools and materials at your fingertips takes the headache out of lesson preparation. Labelled empty photocopy paper boxes or plastic tubs in a central location are very functional. Stack them neatly along a wall. Enlist adult or parent help to set up and maintain your resources.

Basic school supplies

- acrylic paint – standard colours and fluorescent
- Edicol™ or vegetable dye
- brushes – small, medium and large
    – glue brushes
- cartridge paper – large, approx. 56 cm x 36 cm
    – medium A3
    – small A4
- litho paper – large, approx. 56 cm x 36 cm
    – medium A3
    – small A4
- coloured card for mounting work (including black)
- coloured paper squares – glossy, matt and fluorescent
- tissue paper
- crepe paper

- string
- glitter – variety of colours
- pipe-cleaners – sparkly
- feathers
- lead pencils/erasers
- glue sticks
- coloured pencils
- wax crayons
- oil pastels
- permanent black markers (e.g. Artline™ 70)
- fine black markers (e.g. Artline™ 200)
- scissors
- A3 portfolio (optional)
- craft glue 250 mL (squeeze bottle)

Useful collectables

- polystyrene trays to use as paint trays
- newspapers
- sponge blocks (offcuts available from foam rubber outlets)
- fabric scraps (students who do dancing often have an abundance of interesting fabric scraps at home)
- cardboard offcuts
- corks
- cereal boxes (both ends opened, then flattened for easy storage)
- utensils – spoons, forks, blunt kitchen knives, whisks
- ice-cream containers
- takeaway food containers
- clay (e.g. Northcote™ terracotta is very child-friendly)
- craft sticks
- masking tape
- strawboard or thick cardboard
- toothpicks
- foil
- plastic sheeting
- overhead transparencies

- liquid detergent
- mineral turpentine (low-odour substitutes are also available)
- hot glue gun and glue sticks
- wool (variety of colours)
- paper cutter
- staplers
- fishing line
- steel wool
- washing up sponges
- egg cartons
- biscuit cutters
- greeting cards
- Easter egg wrappers
- fur offcuts (pref. 'faux' fur)
- bubble wrap
- plastic bottle tops
- birthday wrapping paper
- curling ribbon
- paint samples
- coloured cupcake papers

Primary art iii

Teachers notes

Each art project is presented over four pages:
- teachers page
- full-colour photograph of completed art project
- student's reflection page
- task assessment

Teachers page

Art project title

Number of lessons included in the art project.

Colour codes identify **visual arts strands** addressed in lesson activities.

Key focus points to promote **discussion** of theme and for effective **lesson preparation**.

Star code to indicate adult help.

Project theme synopsis

Simple, multiskilled **art activities** with effective results.

Material requirements appropriate to each lesson. Activities make use of easily accessible resources/mediums.

Rainbow iceblocks on sticks

This project was inspired by the theme *Summer*.

Three-lesson project

Discussion points
- What are the four seasons? (summer, autumn, winter, spring)
- In which season do we most enjoy having cold treats? (summer—when the weather is warmer.)
- What is your favourite cold summer treat? (icy poles, ice-cream, chilled fruit etc.)
- Why is an ice-cream a treat and not a healthy food? (lots of sugar; emphasise that ice-creams are a treat and we should only eat them occasionally)
- What are the primary colours? (red, blue, yellow) If desired, revise colour mixing of primary colours. Red and blue make purple, blue and yellow make green, yellow and red make orange.

Lesson one
Materials
- A3 cartridge paper (2 sheets per child)
- wax crayons
- Edicol™ or vegetable dye (primary colours)
- paintbrushes (medium)
- newspaper to protect workspace
- coloured card for mounting background
- craft glue for mounting

Method
1. Following discussion, with A3 cartridge paper in landscape position, demonstrate painting with dye, using the three primary colours. Paint very wet horizontal stripes. Commence with yellow, then red, then blue. Hold work vertically to allow colours to run together in a rainbow of colour.
2. Students complete the process to make their own artwork. Set aside to dry.
3. Locate a rough, textured surface.
4. Using wax crayon, rub crayon over second sheet of A3 cartridge paper while leaning on rough surface to create a texture rubbing.
5. Using a contrasting primary colour, paint with dye over texture rubbing. Set aside to dry.
★ 6. Enlist adult help to mount texture rubbing background onto coloured card before Lesson two.

Lesson two
Materials
- artwork in progress
★ - prepared iceblock shape template (page 135)
- cereal box cardboard
- craft sticks
- craft glue
- newspaper to protect workspace
- scissors
- glue stick
- permanent black marker

Method
1. Using glue stick generously, glue rainbow coloured paper onto cereal box cardboard.
2. Using prepared template and permanent black marker, trace four iceblock shapes onto the cereal box cardboard.
3. Cut out shapes and attach craft sticks, using craft glue, to the back of iceblock shapes. Set aside to dry.

Lesson three
Materials
- artwork in progress
- craft glue (squeeze bottle)
- lead pencil
- coloured pencils
- reflection and assessment photocopies

Method
1. Arrange iceblocks on background.
2. Using craft glue, attach iceblocks to background.
3. Students complete reflection activity.
4. Teacher completes assessment record.

114 *Primary art*

R.I.C. Publications/Prim-Ed Publishing

Completed art project

Art project title

Rainbow iceblocks on sticks

Primary art

115

Clear, full-colour **photograph** of completed art project.

R.I.C. Publications/Prim-Ed Publishing

Teachers notes

Student reflection sheet

Related **art project title**

Objective and meaningful lesson **reflections**. Each provides a **self-analysis** of a student's **performance** for each key lesson point.

Task assessment sheet

Related art project **title**

Outcome strands identified for each art project.

Task identified for **assessment** for each art project.

Assessment key

Identified **task criteria**. Task assessment sheets provide a quick means to identify and record a student's performance in criteria which assess the given outcomes.

Primary art ▼

The colour wheel

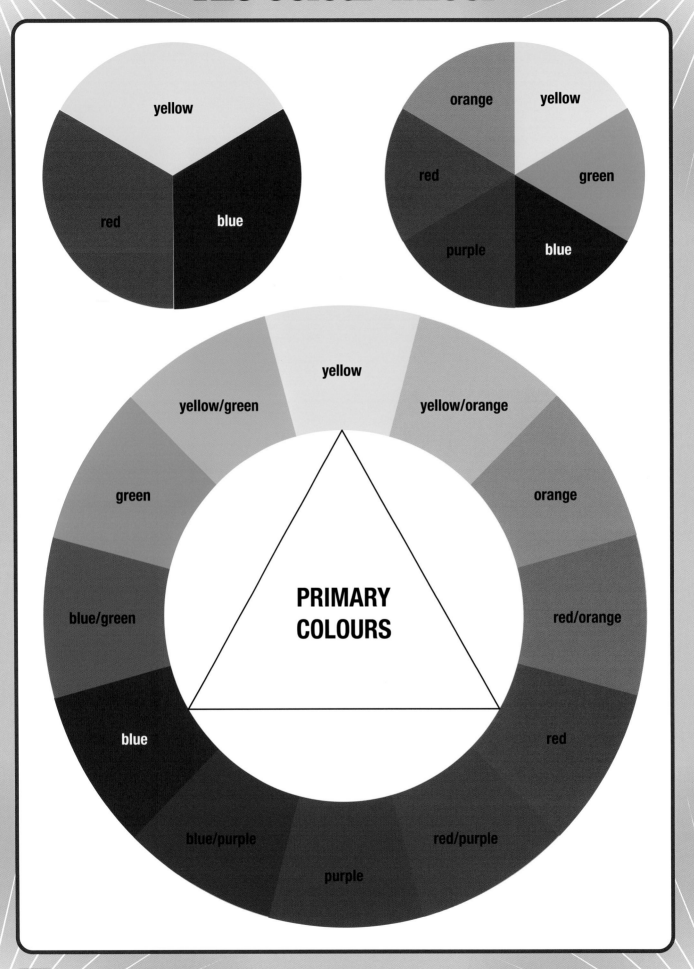

The colour wheel glossary

Hues

Variety of colours.

Primary colours

red, yellow and **blue**

These colours may be blended/mixed to make all other colours except white and black.

Secondary colours

orange, green and **purple**

These colours are created when two primary colours are blended/mixed.

red + yellow = orange

yellow + blue = green

blue + red = purple

Intermediate colours

These colours are created by mixing one primary and one secondary colour.

red–orange

yellow–orange

yellow–green

blue–green

blue–purple

red–purple

Tertiary colours

These colours do not appear on the colour wheel and are created when any three primary colours are blended/mixed together in varying quantities.

Neutrals

White, black and **grey** (White for tints and black for shades.)

Tints

Tinting is a process where white is added to a base colour. Colours created are generally known as pastel colours. Large quantities of white are required to change a colour significantly.

Shades

Shades are created by adding black to a base colour. Only small amounts of black are required to make a base colour darker.

Complementary colours

These colours are opposites on the colour wheel. They are a strong contrast and stand out when adjacent to each other.

R.I.C. Publications/Prim-Ed Publishing

Busy frog pond

This lesson may be related to several themes including *Life cycles, Environmental studies, Looking after our waterways* etc.

Three-lesson project

Discussion points

- What do we find in a pond? (e.g. lily pads, water, tadpoles, frogs, fish etc.)
- What are baby frogs called? (tadpoles)
- Why do you think many frogs have a greenish colour? (to blend in with their surroundings — camouflage)
- What do frogs eat? (small fish and insects — mosquitoes, dragonflies etc.)
- What noise does a frog make? (croak, ribbit etc.)
- What do insects, small fish and frogs in a pond do? (buzz around, eat, swim etc.)
- What is pollution? (damaging the air, land or water with dangerous substances)
- What can we do to stop ponds from becoming polluted? (Put rubbish in the bin; if we see rubbish near a pond, ask Mum or Dad if we can put it in the bin etc.)

Lesson one

Materials

- A3 cartridge paper
- A4 cartridge paper
- blue paint
- green paint
- sponges
- polystyrene trays (for paint)
- wax crayons/oil pastels
- permanent black marker
- lead pencil
- newspaper to protect workspace
- card for mounting
- craft glue for mounting

Method

1. Following discussion about frogs and their environment, use wax crayons to draw lily pads and weeds with strong, solid lines on A3 cartridge paper.
2. Lightly sponge water blue and lily pads green. Emphasise 'pat and lift' technique (no dragging). Set aside to dry.
3. Using permanent black marker, complete a step-by-step drawing of a frog on A4 paper (see steps).
4. Using green and brown oil pastels, randomly colour sections on the frog.
5. Using index finger, gently smudge colours to make a mottled effect (camouflage).
★ 6. Enlist adult helper to mount A3 background onto coloured card before Lesson two.

Lesson two

Materials

- artwork in progress
- permanent black marker
- craft glue
- paintbrush (fine)
- glitter (silver and blue)
- polystyrene tray (for craft glue)
- small polystyrene blocks to slightly elevate frog from picture
- lead pencil
- scrap white paper
- scissors
- glue stick
- hot glue gun (optional)
- newspaper to protect workspace

Method

1. Using permanent black marker, practise drawing dragonflies on scrap paper. When satisfied, draw three dragonflies on the background.
2. Using fine paintbrush and craft glue, paint wings on dragonflies.
3. Sprinkle with silver glitter.
4. To create an illusion of movement, paint small curved lines around dragonflies with craft glue.
5. Sprinkle with blue glitter.
★ 6. Using hot glue gun, glue three small blocks of polystyrene onto the back of cut out frog. Hot glue frog onto picture. (Craft glue may be substituted for hot glue.)

Lesson three

Materials

- reflection and assessment photocopies
- lead pencil
- coloured pencils

Method

1. Students complete reflection activity.
2. Teacher completes assessment record.

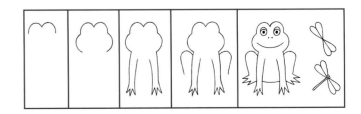

Busy frog pond

Busy frog pond

Reflections

1. List six things you are likely to find in, or near, a pond.

_____

_____

2. Circle the part of the activity you enjoyed most.

drawing the lily pads and leaves with wax crayon

sponge painting the lily pads and water with acrylic paint

drawing the frog with permanent black marker

completing the frog by colouring and smudging oil pastels

cutting out the frog

drawing the dragonflies

adding glitter to enhance your picture

3. Put a tick on the things you used to make your picture.

scissors	oil pastels	glue stick	black marker	cartridge paper
lead pencil	wax crayons	craft glue	dye	glitter
green paint	blue paint	paintbrushes	polystyrene blocks	sponges

4. What can we do to help protect ponds from becoming polluted?

_____

_____

5. Draw three things a frog would like to eat. Colour your drawing with pencils.

R.I.C. Publications/Prim-Ed Publishing

Busy frog pond
Task assessment

Activity objectives
Arts ideas: *Creates artworks to express ideas.*
Arts skills and processes: *Uses a range of visual arts skills, techniques, procedures, practices and technologies.*
Arts responses: *Uses an aesthetic understanding to acknowledge, reflect on and assess the arts.*
Arts in society: *Demonstrates an understanding of the part that the arts play in society.*

Task
The students were instructed to make a 'frog pond' picture using a range of skills, techniques, mediums and materials.

Assessment key			
✔ **yes** (has demonstrated achievement of this criterion)			
✗ **no** (has not demonstrated achievement of this criterion)			
● **inconsistent** (some evidence of achievement has been shown)			
Criteria			
The student is able to:	✔	✗	●
participate in class discussion about frogs and their environment.			
demonstrate strong, solid colouring when using wax crayons to draw lily pads and weeds.			
sponge paint using a 'pat and lift' technique.			
complete a step-by-step drawing of a frog.			
draw dragonflies using permanent black marker.			
enhance picture with glitter highlights.			
complete a reflection sheet based on his/her artwork.			
listen to and follow instructions.			
work cooperatively in an informal activity-based work environment.			

Crazy creations

This project was inspired by 'the fauves', a group of French artists who painted real-life scenes in unexpected colours (for example; purple people, red grass).

This is basically a free painting activity. The scene demonstrated/modelled is a beach scene, but the children were encouraged to create any 'real-life' scene which would enable them to demonstrate effective colour changes.

Two-lesson project

Discussion points

- Have you ever seen red grass?
- Have you ever seen a purple person?
- Have you ever seen a green cat? What would our world look like if things weren't the colours we expected them to be? (We are going to find out.) Mention 'the fauves' and their unusual way of creating 'the unexpected' in their artwork.

Lesson one

Materials

- A3 cartridge paper
- A4 scrap paper
- acrylic paints (variety of colours)
- large lithograph paper (for demonstration/modelling)
- permanent black marker (for demonstration/modelling)
- paintbrushes (medium and fine)
- polystyrene trays (for paint)
- wax crayons
- lead pencil
- newspaper to protect workspace
- card for mounting
- craft glue for mounting

Method

1. Following discussion about 'the fauves', complete the following modelling activity:

   On a large sheet of lithograph paper, using a permanent black marker, draw a plan of a beach scene, including a pet dog (see example). Label parts of picture with colours intended for painting. The sand is red, the dog is green, the sky is yellow, the sun is green, beach towel and football are silver, palm tree trunk is orange, leaves are fluoro pink and the grass is blue.

2. Students use lead pencil on A4 paper and draw a plan of a 'real-life' scene, labelling picture with intended colours.

3. Using lead pencil, lightly transfer plan onto A3 cartridge paper.

4. Using wax crayons, colour small areas; e.g. dog.

5. Using paints and medium or fine paintbrushes, paint 'fauve'-influenced scene. Set aside to dry.

★ 6. Enlist adult help to mount pictures onto coloured card before Lesson two.

Lesson two

Materials

- artwork in progress
- permanent black marker
- reflection and assessment photocopies
- lead pencil
- coloured pencils

Method

1. Using a permanent black marker, highlight detail in picture.

2. Students complete reflection activity.

3. Teacher completes assessment record.

Crazy creations
Reflections

1. *Circle the mediums, materials and tools used to make your picture.*

wax crayons   cartridge paper
coloured paper   paint
tissue paper   cardboard
lead pencil   permanent black marker

2. *Did you find your plan useful? Yes/No (Give a reason for your answer.)*

_____

_____

3. *List the things you painted in your 'real to life' scene. Next to each, print the colour that you used; e.g. people, purple.*

_____ _____

_____ _____

_____ _____

_____ _____

_____ _____

4. *Using lead pencil, draw a different plan for a 'crazy creation' picture. Colour your picture with pencils.*

Crazy creations
Task assessment

Activity objectives

Arts ideas: *Creates artworks to express ideas.*

Arts skills and processes: *Uses a range of visual arts skills, techniques, procedures, practices and technologies.*

Arts responses: *Uses an aesthetic understanding to acknowledge, reflect on and assess the arts.*

Arts in society: *Demonstrates an understanding of the part that the arts play in society.*

Task

The students were instructed to make a picture with a 'fauve' influence, using a range of skills, techniques and materials.

Assessment key			
✔ **yes** (has demonstrated achievement of this criterion)			
✗ **no** (has not demonstrated achievement of this criterion)			
● **inconsistent** (some evidence of achievement has been shown)			
Criteria			
The student is able to:	✔	✗	●
participate in discussion about 'fauve' influence.			
draw a picture plan using lead pencil.			
transfer picture plan onto A3 cartridge paper.			
colour small detail in picture with wax crayon.			
brush paint with paints.			
paint a picture using unexpected colours.			
complete a reflection sheet based on his/her artwork.			
listen to and follow instructions.			
work cooperatively in an informal activity-based work environment.			

Primary art **9**

Spring is in the air

This lesson was inspired by the theme *Spring*. Flowers can be related to a wide range of themes; e.g. celebrations, seasons and colour.

Three-lesson project

Discussion points

- A vase of flowers or photos/posters of flowers will inspire discussion.
- In which season of the year do most flowers bloom? (spring)
- Where do most plants with flowers grow? (in sunny places)
- What flowers have you noticed in gardens?
- What colours are the blooms you have seen?
- Do the petals have colour variations?
- Do you have flowering plants at home?
- Can you name some flowering plants?
- What insects have you noticed among the flowers in your garden? (ants, mosquitoes, dragonflies, bees, butterflies etc.)
- What do plants need to grow? (air, soil, water)
- What is it about flowers people like? (their beauty, scent, bright and colourful, they attract insects and birds etc.)
- What do we use flowers for? (to add colour to enhance our surroundings, to enjoy in the garden, as gifts etc.)

Lesson one

Materials

- A3 cartridge paper
- A4 cartridge paper
- green wax crayons
- bright green dye
- paintbrush (medium)
- newspaper to protect workspace
- coloured card for mounting
- craft glue for mounting

Method

1. Following discussion about flowering plants, students use green wax crayons to draw strong, solid line spirals and curved lines (to represent a vine-type image) on A3 cartridge paper.
2. Using green wax crayons, draw four leaf shapes (widthwise) onto A4 paper. Draw leaf vein markings. Emphasise strong, solid lines to create a resistance to the dye.
3. Using green dye, paint over wax crayon drawings. Set aside to dry.
★ 4. Enlist adult help to mount background onto coloured card before Lesson two.

Lesson two

Materials

- artwork in progress
- coloured paper
★ - prepared petal shape and flower centre templates (page 123)
- lead pencil
- scissors
- glue stick
- newspaper to protect workspace

Method

1. Using prepared petal shape template and lead pencil, students trace five petal shapes and one flower centre onto the wrong side of coloured paper.
2. Cut out petals, flower centre and leaf shapes.
3. Arrange petals and leaves into position on background.
★ 4. Enlist adult help to assist children.
   Starting at the centre of the flowers, glue petals into position using generous swipes of glue stick. Gently push outer point of petal towards the centre to create a 3-D effect. (Generous application of glue will ensure petals adhere.)
5. Using generous swipes of glue stick, glue leaves into position.
6. Glue centre circle onto flower.

Lesson three

Materials

- reflection and assessment photocopies
- lead pencil
- coloured pencils

Method

1. Students complete reflection activity.
2. Teacher completes assessment record.

R.I.C. Publications/Prim-Ed Publishing

Spring is in the air

Reflections

1. Colour the tools, mediums and materials used to make your picture.

sponges	paint	dye
paintbrush	wax crayons	coloured pencils
oil pastels	cardboard templates	pompom
coloured paper	scissors	glue stick
craft glue	coloured cardboard	glitter

2. Circle the part of the activity you enjoyed most.

drawing solid wax crayon lines to represent vines and leaves

painting over the wax crayon drawings with dye

tracing the petal and flower centre templates

cutting out the flower centre, petals and leaf shapes

arranging and gluing the flower parts onto the background

3. Why did you enjoy this part of the activity the most?

_____

_____

_____

_____

_____

4. In which season do most flowering plants bloom? _____

5. Who would appreciate receiving your art as a gift?

_____

Give a reason for your answer.

_____

_____

_____

_____

R.I.C. Publications/Prim-Ed Publishing

Spring is in the air

Task assessment

Activity objectives

Arts ideas: *Creates artworks to express ideas.*

Arts skills and processes: *Uses a range of visual arts skills, techniques, procedures, practices and technologies.*

Arts responses: *Uses an aesthetic understanding to acknowledge, reflect on and assess the arts.*

Arts in society: *Demonstrates an understanding of the part that the arts play in society.*

Task

The students were instructed to make a 3-D picture of a 'spring flower' using a range of skills, techniques, mediums and materials.

Assessment key			
✔ **yes** (has demonstrated achievement of this criterion)			
✗ **no** (has not demonstrated achievement of this criterion)			
● **inconsistent** (some evidence of achievement has been shown)			
Criteria			
The student is able to:	✔	✗	●
participate in class discussion about spring and flowers.			
demonstrate drawing strong, solid lines using wax crayons.			
paint over wax crayon drawings with dye.			
trace prepared templates.			
position and glue flower parts and leaves into place.			
complete a reflection sheet based on his/her artwork.			
listen to and follow instructions.			
work cooperatively in an informal activity-based work environment.			

All seasons leaning board

This project was inspired by the topic *The seasons*. The theme of *The seasons* covers the whole year and makes the leaning board appropriate throughout the academic year. (Note: A leaning board is a protective board similar to a placemat.)

Two-lesson project

Discussion points

- What are the seasons? (summer, autumn, winter and spring)
- What sort of weather do we experience in summer? (hot, dry weather) autumn? (warm, cool weather) winter? (cold, wet weather) spring? (cool, warm weather)
- Discuss weather-appropriate characteristics for each season; e.g. summer, very hot, swimming at the beach; autumn, leaves falling from the trees; winter, walking in the rain with an umbrella; spring, flowers blooming.

Lesson one

Materials

★ • A3 cartridge paper (trim 2 cm from a length side and 2 cm from a width side)
- permanent black marker
- wax crayons
- oil pastels
- lead pencil
- newspaper to protect workspace
- A3 laminating sheets

Method

1. Following discussion about the seasons, students use permanent black marker to draw four pictures on a sheet of A3 cartridge paper, each of which represent one of the four seasons.
2. Using wax crayons and oil pastels, colour pictures. Emphasise strong, solid colour.
3. To fill in background, draw strong, solid scribbles using oil pastels.
★ 4. Enlist adult help to laminate completed leaning boards.

Lesson two

Materials

- reflection and assessment photocopies
- lead pencils
- coloured pencils

Method

1. Students complete reflection activity.
2. Teacher completes assessment record.

R.I.C. Publications/Prim-Ed Publishing

All seasons leaning board

Reflections

1. *Colour the mediums, materials and tools used to make your leaning board.*

wax crayons	scissors	lead pencil
paintbrush	coloured paper	cartridge paper
dye	oil pastels	paint
glitter	magazines	glue stick

2. *Circle the part of the activity you enjoyed most.*

drawing the pictures representing the four seasons

colouring the pictures with oil pastels and wax crayons

colouring the background with strong, solid squiggles

3. *Why did you enjoy this the most?*

_____

_____

4. *Using lead pencil, draw an 'all seasons' picture showing outdoor activities you would do in each season. Colour your picture with pencils.*

All seasons leaning board

Task assessment

Activity objectives

Arts ideas: *Creates artworks to express ideas.*

Arts skills and processes: *Uses a range of visual arts skills, techniques, procedures, practices and technologies.*

Arts responses: *Uses an aesthetic understanding to acknowledge, reflect on and assess the arts.*

Arts in society: *Demonstrates an understanding of the part that the arts play in society.*

Task

The students were instructed to make a 'leaning board' using a range of skills, techniques, mediums and materials.

Assessment key			
✔ **yes** (has demonstrated achievement of this criterion)			
✗ **no** (has not demonstrated achievement of this criterion)			
● **inconsistent** (some evidence of achievement has been shown)			
Criteria			
The student is able to:	✔	✗	●
participate in discussion about the seasons and characteristics of each.			
use permanent black marker to draw four pictures representing the four seasons.			
demonstrate strong, solid colouring while completing the four pictures and background.			
complete a reflection sheet based on his/her artwork.			
listen to and follow instructions.			
work cooperatively in an informal activity-based work environment.			

Origami fish scene

This project was inspired by the theme *The sea*. It incorporates an environmental message about protecting our sea life from extinction.

Three-lesson project

Discussion points

Stimulus pictures of colourful tropical fish would be helpful.

- What have you noticed about the colours of 'tropical fish'? (very bright and colourful)
- Why do you think 'tropical fish' have bright colours? (camouflage to live among the bright coral)
- What is a habitat? (the natural environment of a plant or animal)
- Lots of people enjoy looking at 'tropical fish'. Popular reefs, which are the habitat for beautiful fish, are under threat by humans.
- What can we do to prevent this environment from being spoiled? (don't leave rubbish when we go to the beach, when boating make sure no rubbish goes overboard etc.)
- If we visit areas to go snorkelling or reef walking, we must obey the rules which keep the habitats safe from damage.

Lesson one

Materials

- A3 cartridge paper
- bright blue dye
- paintbrush (medium)
- permanent black marker
- wax crayons/oil pastels
- sea salt
- lead pencil
- card for mounting
- craft glue for mounting
- newspaper to protect workspace

Method

1. Following discussion about tropical fish and their habitat, students draw weeds onto paper using permanent black marker.
2. Colour weeds with wax crayons or oil pastels using strong, solid colour.
3. Paint around weeds with blue dye.
4. Sprinkle lightly with sea salt while wet to create a speckled/bubbled effect. Set aside to dry.
★ 5. Enlist adult help to mount backgrounds before Lesson two.

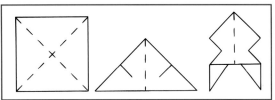

Lesson two

Materials

- artwork in progress
★ • cartridge paper squares (21 cm x 21 cm) and (10 cm x 10 cm)
★ • origami paper (bright colours) (15 cm x 15 cm)
- wax crayons or oil pastels
- dye
- paintbrushes (medium and fine)
- scissors
- craft glue
- polystyrene trays (for glue)
- goggle eyes (optional)
- glitter
- newspaper to protect workspace

Method

1. Demonstrate step-by-step paper folding of origami fish (see below).
2. Students make three fish of varying sizes.
3. Decorate cartridge paper fish with wax crayon or oil pastel patterns. Emphasise solid colouring.
4. Paint dye around patterns and set aside to dry.
5. Using fine paintbrush, paint craft glue detail and sprinkle with glitter.
6. Using craft glue, attach goggle eyes. (If goggle eyes are not available, a circle drawn on white paper works well.) Draw pupil detail with permanent black marker.

Lesson three

Materials

- artwork in progress
- glue stick
★ • tissue paper (light and dark green strips approx 3 cm x 30 cm)
- lead pencil
- coloured pencils
- reflection and assessment photocopies

Method

1. Randomly twist tissue paper and glue into position on background.
2. Position fish onto background and glue in place with glue stick.
3. Students complete reflection activity.
4. Teacher completes assessment record.

Origami fish scene

R.I.C. Publications/Prim-Ed Publishing

Origami fish scene

Reflections

1. Colour the mediums, materials and tools used to make your picture.

wax crayons	cartridge paper	coloured paper
paint	salt	dye
oil pastels	glitter	small shells
flat-ended pencil	permanent black marker	cardboard
tissue paper	glue stick	goggle eyes

2. Which part of this activity did you enjoy the most?
   Why? _____

   _____

3. What is a habitat?_____

   _____

4. List two things we can do to prevent tropical fish from becoming extinct.

   _____

   _____

5. Draw a tropical fish safely camouflaged among some coral.
   Colour your drawing using pencils.

Origami fish scene

Task assessment

Activity objectives

Arts ideas: *Creates artworks to express ideas.*

Arts skills and processes: *Uses a range of visual arts skills, techniques, procedures, practices and technologies.*

Arts responses: *Uses an aesthetic understanding to acknowledge, reflect on and assess the arts.*

Arts in society: *Demonstrates an understanding of the part that the arts play in society.*

Task

The students were instructed to make an origami fish scene using a range of skills, techniques, mediums and materials.

Assessment key
✔ **yes** (has demonstrated achievement of this criterion)
✗ **no** (has not demonstrated achievement of this criterion)
● **inconsistent** (some evidence of achievement has been shown)

Criteria			
The student is able to:	✔	✗	●
participate in class discussion about tropical fish and their habitat.			
demonstrate solid colouring using oil pastels or wax crayons.			
paint background using dye.			
follow steps to make an origami fish.			
decorate cartridge paper fish using oil pastels or wax crayons and dye.			
twist tissue paper strips to make seaweed.			
add detail to fish using craft glue and glitter.			
glue tissue paper seaweed into position.			
glue fish into position.			
complete a reflection sheet based on his/her artwork.			
listen to and follow instructions.			
work cooperatively in an informal activity-based work environment.			

Primary art **21**

Fancy fish plaques

This lesson was inspired by the theme *The sea*. It involves simple techniques and is an excellent introduction to the awareness of textures. The finished project makes a lovely garden or wall plaque suitable for a gift.

Two-lesson project

Discussion points

If possible, stimulus pictures of fish are an excellent resource to enable children to see the parts of a fish clearly.

- What animals live in the sea? (crayfish, crabs, jellyfish, fish etc.)
- What do fish look like? (have a head, tail, fins, scales etc.)
- What do we do with fish? (eat them, admire them in fish tanks etc.)

Lesson one

Materials

- terracotta clay (a large fist-sized piece per child)
- ★ prepared fish shape template (page 124)
- newspaper to protect workspace
- rolling pin (or conduit lengths)
- cardboard work surface (This may be a piece of card from packaging.)
- craft stick
- large nail
- drinking straw
- cord or string to hang plaque
- tools (such as pens etc. for making textures)

Method

1. Following discussion about the sea and fish, students use straight fingers and flat palms to roll rolling pin over the clay in a rolling motion on cardboard work surface.
2. Roll clay to about $^3/_4$ cm to 1 cm thickness.
3. Place fish template onto the clay.
4. Cut around template using a craft stick.
5. Using arbitrary tools, press textures into the clay. (The end of a craft stick makes excellent rows of scales. Marker pen tops make an excellent eye shape. Use cut down craft sticks to make fin and tail markings. Etched lines can be made using a nail.)
6. Twist straw into clay to extract clay for a hole to thread cord through when project is completed.
7. Remove completed fish from cardboard work surface and air dry approximately one week.
8. Fire terracotta clay or bake.
★ 9. Enlist adult help to attach cord/string.

Lesson two

Materials

- lead pencil
- coloured pencils
- reflection and assessment photocopies

Method

1. Students complete reflection activity.
2. Teacher completes assessment record.

Fancy fish plaques

Reflections

1. *Colour the mediums, materials and tools used to make your 'fancy fish'.*

wax crayons	terracotta clay	fish-shaped template
craft stick	lead pencil	felt pens
large nail	paint	newspaper

2. *Circle the part of this activity you enjoyed most and say why.*

rolling the clay

cutting the fish shape using a craft stick

using tools to press textures into the clay

twisting the straw to make a hole in the clay

_____

_____

3. *Where could you display your 'fancy fish' plaque?*

_____

4. *Use lead pencil to draw another plaque. Add colour with pencils.*

R.I.C. Publications/Prim-Ed Publishing

Fancy fish plaques
Task assessment

Activity objectives

Arts ideas: *Creates artworks to express ideas.*

Arts skills and processes: *Uses a range of visual arts skills, techniques, procedures, practices and technologies.*

Arts responses: *Uses an aesthetic understanding to acknowledge, reflect on and assess the arts.*

Arts in society: *Demonstrates an understanding of the part that the arts play in society.*

Task

The students were instructed to make 'fish plaques' using a range of skills, techniques, mediums and materials.

Assessment key			
✔ **yes** *(has demonstrated achievement of this criterion)*			
✘ **no** *(has not demonstrated achievement of this criterion)*			
● **inconsistent** *(some evidence of achievement has been shown)*			
Criteria			
The student is able to:	✔	✘	●
participate in class discussion about the sea and fish.			
use a rolling motion and a rolling pin to roll clay to a thickness of approximately one centimetre.			
use a craft stick to cut around fish-shaped template.			
make textures in the clay using arbitrary tools.			
twist a straw into clay to make a hole for display purposes.			
complete a reflection sheet based on his/her artwork.			
listen to and follow instructions.			
work cooperatively in an informal activity-based work environment.			

Leaping lizards

This lesson was inspired by the theme *Reptiles*, with an emphasis on their characteristic of camouflage.

Three-lesson project

Discussion points

- What are reptiles?
- How are they different from people? (They are cold-blooded and people are warm-blooded.)
- What do lizards eat? (Depending on type of lizard and their size, some eat insects, eggs and other small animals.)
- What colours are they? (They tend to blend in with their environment; i.e. use camouflage.)
- Where do they live? (Usually in warm places because they need the sun's warmth to be active. This is why we see more snakes and lizards in hot countries.)
- How do they blend into their surroundings? (Some lizards can change colour to match their surroundings.)

Lesson one

Materials

- A3 cartridge paper
- A4 cartridge paper
- ★ prepared lizard-shaped template (page 125)
- wax crayons or oil pastels
- acrylic paint (greens, brown, blue and silver)
- polystyrene trays (for paint)
- ★ strips of coloured paper (approx 2 cm wide)—blues and greens
- scissors
- glue stick
- craft glue for mounting
- coloured card for mounting work
- lead pencil
- newspaper to protect workspace
- sponges

Method

1. Following discussion about reptiles, lizards and camouflage, students use wax crayons or oil pastels to draw a large leaf shape on A3 cartridge paper. Emphasise strong, solid lines.
2. Using a sponge and light green paint, sponge leaf using a 'pat and lift' technique (no dragging).
3. Using dark green paint, sponge paint around leaf shape.
4. Using a dry sponge and a very small amount of brown, silver and blue paint, lightly sponge over the top of the background area around the leaf. (Some children will be heavy-handed but this adds character and variation between paintings.)
★ 5. Set aside to dry. Enlist adult help to mount background onto coloured card before Lesson two.

6. Using lead pencil, trace prepared lizard template onto A4 cartridge paper.
7. Cut paper strips into squares.
8. Using glue stick, attach squares to lizard shape to create a mosaic effect.
9. To make feet, cut squares into triangles as shown in example.

Lesson two

Materials

- artwork in progress
- materials required to complete stages commenced in Lesson one
- green scrap paper
- permanent black marker
- small coin
- scissors
- polystyrene pieces (packaging is suitable—approximately 1 cm thick)
- craft knife
- craft glue (squeeze bottle)
- lead pencil
- newspaper to protect workspace

Method

1. Complete mosaic on lizard.
2. Cut around the outline of the lizard.
3. Using lead pencil, trace coin onto the back of coloured paper.
4. Cut tracing in half and draw eye detail using permanent black marker.
5. Glue eyes into position.
6. Using craft glue, attach three polystyrene pieces at even intervals on the back of the lizard along the centre. Set aside to dry.

Lesson three

Materials

- artwork in progress
- glue stick
- craft glue (squeeze bottle)
- reflection and assessment photocopies
- lead pencil
- coloured pencils

Method

1. Using craft glue, attach polystyrene blocks/lizard onto background
2. Using glue stick, glue feet of lizard onto leaf, so that the lizard is slightly elevated from picture.
3. Students complete reflection activity.
4. Teacher completes assessment record.

R.I.C. Publications/Prim-Ed Publishing

R.I.C. Publications/Prim-Ed Publishing

Leaping lizards

Reflections

1. Colour the mediums, materials and tools used to make your picture.

wax crayons	bark	scissors
coloured paper	coin	paint
glue stick	dye	sponges
permanent black marker	leaf template	oil pastels

2. Circle the part of the activity you enjoyed most.

drawing the leaf shape using wax crayons or oil pastels

sponging the background

tracing the lizard template

cutting out the eyes and lizard shape

colouring the lizard using a mosaic technique

tracing the coin to make the eyes

gluing the eyes onto the lizard and the lizard onto the background

3. Tick the colours you used for your lizard.

red	orange	yellow	brown
purple	green	blue	black

4. Use lead pencil to draw a lizard with different markings. Colour the lizard with pencils. Draw the background in similar colours to camouflage your lizard.

R.I.C. Publications/Prim-Ed Publishing

Leaping lizards

Task assessment

Activity objectives

Arts ideas: *Creates artworks to express ideas.*

Arts skills and processes: *Uses a range of visual arts skills, techniques, procedures, practices and technologies.*

Arts responses: *Uses an aesthetic understanding to acknowledge, reflect on and assess the arts.*

Arts in society: *Demonstrates an understanding of the part that the arts play in society.*

Task

The students were instructed to make a 'leaping lizard' picture using a range of skills, techniques, mediums and materials.

Assessment key			
✔ **yes** *(has demonstrated achievement of this criterion)*			
✗ **no** *(has not demonstrated achievement of this criterion)*			
● **inconsistent** *(some evidence of achievement has been shown)*			
Criteria			
The student is able to:	✔	✗	●
participate in class discussion about reptiles, lizards and camouflage.			
draw a leaf shape using wax crayons or oil pastels, and strong, solid lines.			
sponge a background and leaf shape using paint and 'pat and lift' technique.			
trace a lizard-shaped template using permanent black marker.			
colour lizard with paper squares to create a mosaic effect.			
cut out lizard shape.			
trace a coin to make eyes.			
cut out eyes and glue them onto lizard.			
draw eye detail using permanent black marker.			
glue lizard onto background.			
complete a reflection sheet based on his/her artwork.			
listen to and follow instructions.			
work cooperatively in an informal activity-based work environment.			

Primary art **29**

Healthy foods and treats collage

This lesson was inspired by a health lesson, *Healthy foods and treats*. The children make a collage of healthy foods and foods that should be eaten in moderation (treats).

The children present oral reports about their artwork to small groups to tell others what their favourite treats and healthy foods are.

Two-lesson project

Discussion points

- What are your favourite foods? (Make a list on the board ... healthy foods on one side, treats on the other.)
- Why should we eat more of the healthy foods than the treats? (Treats are often high in fats and/or sugar.)
- Why is it important not to have too much fat or sugar? (Our body is like a machine and we must use good fuel or it won't run efficiently. Too much fat or sugar can have unhealthy consequences, such as diabetes and obesity.) Emphasise that it is okay to have less healthy foods in moderation.

Lesson one

Materials

- A3 cartridge paper
- magazines
- advertising flyers or catalogues
- scissors
- glue stick
- newspaper to protect workspace

Method

1. Following discussion about healthy foods and treats, the students go through magazines and advertising mail, tearing out pictures of their favourite foods. Encourage a balance of healthy foods and treats.
2. Cut out pictures.
3. Fold A3 cartridge paper in half.
4. Arrange pictures on A3 paper with treats on one half of the page and healthy foods on the other. (Children love the game of hiding a very small picture of one of their favourite foods in the collage and challenging people to find it.)
5. Glue pictures into position. Emphasise gluing all edges down.

Lesson two

Materials

- artwork in progress
- oil pastels
- newspaper to protect workspace
- craft glue for mounting
- coloured card for mounting
- lead pencil
- coloured pencils
- reflection and assessment photocopies

Method

1. Add colour to any white paper 'gaps' with two oil pastel colours (not black), using a backwards and forwards drawing motion.
2. In small groups, give students one minute each to talk about their favourite foods and treats while showing their completed collage.
★ 3. Enlist adult help to mount completed work onto coloured card.
4. Students complete reflection activity.
5. Teacher completes assessment record.

Healthy foods and treats collage

Reflections

1. Circle the part of the activity you enjoyed most.

finding the pictures of 'healthy foods' and 'treats'

cutting out the pictures of 'healthy foods' and 'treats'

arranging the pictures onto A3 paper

gluing the pictures onto A3 paper

showing your collage to others and talking about your favourite foods and treats

2. Why did you enjoy this part of the activity?

_____

_____

3. Colour the mediums, materials and tools used to make your picture.

oil pastels	craft glue	magazines	advertising mail
paint	glue stick	scissors	sponges

4. Why is it important to eat more 'healthy foods' than 'treats'?

_____

_____

5. Use a lead pencil to draw your two favourite 'healthy foods' and 'treats'.
   Colour your pictures with pencils.

R.I.C. Publications/Prim-Ed Publishing

Healthy foods and treats collage
Task assessment

Activity objectives
Arts ideas: *Creates artworks to express ideas.*
Arts skills and processes: *Uses a range of visual arts skills, techniques, procedures, practices and technologies.*
Arts responses: *Uses an aesthetic understanding to acknowledge, reflect on and assess the arts.*
Arts in society: *Demonstrates an understanding of the part that the arts play in society.*

Task
The students were instructed to make a 'healthy food and treats' collage using a range of skills and materials.

Assessment key			
✔ **yes** *(has demonstrated achievement of this criterion)*			
✗ **no** *(has not demonstrated achievement of this criterion)*			
● **inconsistent** *(some evidence of achievement has been shown)*			
Criteria			
The student is able to:	✔	✗	●
participate in class discussion about 'healthy foods and treats'.			
look through magazines and advertising mail to select relevant pictures.			
cut out pictures.			
fold A3 paper in half.			
arrange 'healthy food' pictures on one half of page and 'treats' on the other half.			
glue pictures into position on A3 paper.			
colour remaining gaps with two oil pastel colours using a backwards and forwards motion.			
talk about his/her favourite 'healthy foods and treats' while showing collage to others.			
complete a reflection sheet based on his/her artwork.			
listen to and follow instructions.			
work cooperatively in an informal activity-based work environment.			

Finger-painted flower card
(Female emphasis)

This card is simple and effective. The decoration can determine its purpose: Mother's Day, birthday, thank you, get well etc.

Three-lesson project

Discussion points

- What is a greeting card?
- Have you ever received a greeting card?
- Why were you given a greeting card?
- Have you ever given someone a greeting card? (List reasons why we have given or received greeting cards – get well, thank you, congratulations, birthday, wedding etc.)
- Why do people like flowers? (colourful, scented, beautiful etc.)
- Who have you seen receiving flowers as a gift? (Answers will vary – mostly females.)
- What are reasons for giving flowers? (a gift; thank you; Mother's Day; birthday; to recognise an achievement such as Commonwealth Games and Olympic medal winners etc.)

Lesson one

Materials

- ★ • *cartridge paper cut to size (13.5 cm x 19 cm)*
- *acrylic paint (variety of colours)*
- *flat-ended pencil (for printing)*
- *matchstick*
- *polystyrene trays (for paint)*
- *lead pencil*
- *newspaper to protect workspace*

Method

1. Following discussion about greeting cards and flowers, demonstrate 'finger painting' techniques – 'drag' technique and 'print' technique (pat and lift).
2. The students paint stem and leaves of a flower using 'finger dragging' technique on cut cartridge paper.
3. Students print flower centres and petal using 'finger prints' ('pat and lift' technique.)
4. Using the flat end of a pencil, print a caterpillar walking somewhere in the picture.
5. Add detail to the caterpillar by using the matchstick to drag or print paint.
6. Students may create their own printed shapes; e.g. a dragonfly. The example shown was 'dragged' and 'printed' with the end of a paperclip. Set aside to dry.

Lesson two

Materials

- *artwork in progress*
- ★ • *coloured card cut to size (14.5 cm x 20 cm) for mounting*
- ★ • *coloured card (31 cm x 21 cm) for greeting card*
- *glue stick*
- *lead pencil or pen to write greeting*
- *newspaper to protect workspace*
- ★ • *optional: glitter glue, glitter pen or glitter. If glitter is being used, a fine brush and craft glue will be necessary.*

Method

1. Using glue stick, attach finger-painted picture onto smaller piece of mounting card.
2. Fold larger coloured card in half to make a greeting card base.
3. Glue mounted picture to the front of the folded greeting card.
4. Write appropriate message on the right-hand inside of card.
5. ★ Enlist adult help to add glitter enhancement and appropriate heading on the front of card; e.g. 'Mum'. Students may do this if desired.

Lesson three

Materials

- *reflection and assessment photocopies*
- *lead pencil*
- *coloured pencils*

Method

1. Students complete reflection activity.
2. Teacher completes assessment record.

Finger-painted flower card

Reflections

1. *Colour the mediums, materials and tools used to make your greeting card.*

cartridge paper	craft glue	coloured paper
scissors	lead pencil	coloured card
paint	matchstick	fine black marker
paperclips	glitter	dye

2. *Circle the part of the activity you enjoyed the most and say why.*

dragging the paint to make the flower stem

finger printing the flower centres and petals

printing a caterpillar using the flat end of a pencil and a matchstick

writing the message in the card

_____

_____

3. *Who did you make your greeting card for?*_____

4. *For what occasion did you make your card?*_____

5. *Use lead pencil to draw another 'flower' picture to put on the front of a greeting card. Colour your picture with pencils.*

*Who would you give this card to?*_____

*Why?*_____

_____

R.I.C. Publications/Prim-Ed Publishing

Finger-painted flower card
Task assessment

Activity objectives

Arts ideas: *Creates artworks to express ideas.*

Arts skills and processes: *Uses a range of visual arts skills, techniques, procedures, practices and technologies.*

Arts responses: *Uses an aesthetic understanding to acknowledge, reflect on and assess the arts.*

Arts in society: *Demonstrates an understanding of the part that the arts play in society.*

Task

The students were instructed to make a flower greeting card using
a range of skills, techniques, mediums and materials.

Assessment key
✔ **yes** *(has demonstrated achievement of this criterion)*
✗ **no** *(has not demonstrated achievement of this criterion)*
● **inconsistent** *(some evidence of achievement has been shown)*

Criteria			
The student is able to:	✔	✗	●
participate in class discussion about greeting cards and flowers.			
demonstrate 'dragging' finger painting technique.			
demonstrate 'finger print' finger painting technique.			
demonstrate 'dragging' and 'printing' using arbitrary tools.			
glue painted picture onto mounting card.			
fold a piece of card in half widthwise.			
glue mounted picture onto folded card.			
write a message in the card.			
complete a reflection sheet based on his/her artwork.			
listen to and follow instructions.			
work cooperatively in an informal activity-based work environment.			

Primary art **37**

Printed garden scene card

(Male emphasis)

This is simple but effective and the decoration can determine its purpose: Father's Day, thank you, get well, congratulations.

Three-lesson project

Discussion points

- What is a greeting card?
- Have you ever received a greeting card?
- Why were you given a greeting card?
- Have you ever given someone a greeting card? (List reasons why we have given or received greeting cards.)
- Why do people like gardens? (colourful, calming, peaceful, beautiful, interesting, mini beasts, birds etc.)
- What things do you like about your garden? (colourful flowers, trees, lots of greenery, interesting mini beasts etc.)
- What needs to be done in the garden to keep it maintained? (trim plants, weed, rake the leaves etc.)
- What can be used to carry leaves and prunings? (wheelbarrow)
- What animals might we see in the garden? (birds, cat, dog etc.)
- What mini beasts can you find in the garden? (caterpillars, bees, butterflies, snails, ants etc.)

Lesson one

Materials

- ★ • *cartridge paper cut to size (14 cm x 19 cm)*
- *acrylic paint (variety of colours)*
- *acrylic paint (metallic bronze)*
- *cereal box card (Students to cut various sizes to suit whatever they are printing.)*
- *paintbrush (fine)*
- *matchstick*
- *flat-ended pencil*
- *permanent black marker (The end is used for printing circles.)*
- *polystyrene trays (for paint)*
- *lead pencil*
- *newspaper to protect workspace*

Method

1. Following discussion about greeting cards and gardens, demonstrate 'printing' techniques using the edge of card, paintbrush handle end, matchstick and fingerprint. **Students are instructed to use a minimum of three arbitrary tools** to print their garden picture.
2. Students print bough, branches and leaves of a tree using 'card edge printing' technique onto cartridge paper.

3. Students print flower centres and petals using pencil end for centres and paintbrush handle end for petals ('press and lift' technique).
4. Using the flat end of a pencil, print a caterpillar walking somewhere in the picture.
5. Add detail to caterpillar by using matchstick to drag or print paint.
6. Students may create their own printed shapes; e.g. a wheelbarrow, bird in the tree, cat, kite. Set aside to dry.

Lesson two

Materials

- *artwork in progress*
- ★ • *coloured card cut to size (15 cm x 20 cm) for mounting card*
- ★ • *coloured card cut to size (32 cm x 21 cm) for greeting card*
- *glue stick*
- *lead pencil or pen to write greeting with*
- *newspaper to protect workspace*
- ★ • *optional: glitter glue, glitter pen or glitter. If glitter is being used, a fine brush and craft glue is necessary.*

Method

1. Using glue stick, glue 'finger-painted' picture onto smaller piece of mounting card
2. Fold coloured card in half to make a greeting card base.
3. Glue mounted picture on the front of the folded greeting card.
4. Write appropriate message on the right-hand inside of the card.
5. ★ Enlist adult to help add glitter enhancement and appropriate heading on the front of card; e.g. 'Dad'. Students may choose to do this.

Lesson three

Materials

- *reflection and assessment photocopies*
- *lead pencil*
- *coloured pencils*

Method

1. Students complete reflection activity.
2. Teacher completes assessment record.

Printed garden scene card

R.I.C. Publications/Prim-Ed Publishing

Printed garden scene card

Reflections

1. Colour the mediums and materials used to make your greeting card.

cartridge paper	craft glue	cardboard	metallic paint
coloured card	paint	glitter	dye

2. Circle the tools used to print your picture.

cardboard	sponges	ruler
pencil end	matchstick	craft stick
scissors	permanent black marker	finger
paperclip	paintbrush handle end	marker lid

3. Which part of this activity did you enjoy the most?_____

   Give a reason for your answer. _____

   _____

4. Did you print an extra feature in your picture?

Yes	No

   If so, what did you print and what did you use to print it?

   _____

5. Use lead pencil to draw another 'garden scene' picture to go on the front of a greeting card.

   Who would you give this card to? _____

   Give a reason for your answer. _____

   _____

R.I.C. Publications/Prim-Ed Publishing

Printed garden scene card
Task assessment

Activity objectives

Arts ideas: *Creates artworks to express ideas.*

Arts skills and processes: *Uses a range of visual arts skills, techniques, procedures, practices and technologies.*

Arts responses: *Uses an aesthetic understanding to acknowledge, reflect on and assess the arts.*

Arts in society: *Demonstrates an understanding of the part that the arts play in society.*

Task

The students were instructed to make a 'garden scene' greeting card using a range of skills, techniques, mediums and materials.

Assessment key			
✔ **yes** *(has demonstrated achievement of this criterion)*			
✗ **no** *(has not demonstrated achievement of this criterion)*			
● **inconsistent** *(some evidence of achievement has been shown)*			
Criteria			
The student is able to:	✔	✗	●
participate in class discussion about greeting cards and gardens.			
demonstrate the use of three arbitrary tools (minimum) to print a garden scene.			
glue printed picture onto mounting card.			
fold a piece of card in half widthwise.			
glue mounted picture onto the front of folded card.			
write a message in the card.			
complete a reflection sheet based on his/her artwork.			
listen to and follow instructions.			
work cooperatively in an informal activity-based work environment.			

Blazing sun

This project was inspired by the theme *Seasons*. (Topic: *Summer*) Sun safety was incorporated into the discussion relating to 'good health practices'.

Two-lesson project

Discussion points

- In which season do we see the sun the most? (summer)
- What sort of weather do we have in summer? (hot, warm, dry etc.)
- What sorts of things do we do outside in summer? (swim, play games/sport, go to the beach, picnics etc.)
- What should we wear to protect ourselves from the sun? (protective clothing, SPF 30 sunscreen, a hat etc.)
- What primary colours mixed together make 'orange'? (yellow and red)

Lesson one

Materials

- *A3 cartridge paper*
- *oil pastels (yellow and red)*
- *orange Edicol™ or vegetable dye*
- *paintbrush (thick)*
- *yellow pearl paint (in a squeeze bottle)*
- *coloured card for mounting work*
- *craft glue for mounting*
- *lead pencil*
- *newspaper to protect workspace*

Method

1. Following discussion about the sun, summer and sun protection, students use yellow and red oil pastels, on A3 cartridge paper, draw consecutive circles of lines going backwards and forwards to create solid colour.
2. Using index finger, drag colour outwards from the centre.
3. Paint orange dye over picture. Set aside to dry.
4. Before lesson two, squiggle yellow pearl paint across picture to enhance 'sun' effect. Set aside to dry.
★ 5. Enlist adult to help to mount pictures.

Lesson two

Materials

- *artwork in progress*
- *craft glue (squeeze bottle)*
- *gold glitter*
- *reflection and assessment photocopies*
- *lead pencil*
- *coloured pencils*

Method

1. Squiggle craft glue across picture to enhance 'sun' effect.
★ 2. Sprinkle with gold glitter. Enlist adult help to assist with sprinkling glitter.
3. Students complete reflection activity.
4. Teacher completes assessment record.

R.I.C. Publications/Prim-Ed Publishing

Blazing sun

Blazing sun

Reflections

1. *Circle the part of the activity you enjoyed the most.*

drawing the circles using oil pastels

smudging the circles using your index finger and dragging the
colour from the centre outwards

painting the dye over the 'blazing sun'

adding the pearl paint to your picture

adding the craft glue and glitter to the picture

2. *Why did you enjoy this part of the activity?*

_____

3. *Why was it important to draw strong, solid lines?*

_____

4. *Colour the techniques you used.*

smudged oil pastel colour blending	sponge painting
painting with dye	finger painting
oil pastel resist	brush painting

5. *Circle the items that may help to protect you from the sun.*

sunscreen   hand lotion

sunglasses   hat

sandals   beach umbrella

lip balm SPF 30   protective shirt

surfboard   protective trousers

6. *Use lead pencil to draw yourself doing something you enjoy in summer. Colour your picture with coloured pencils.*

R.I.C. Publications/Prim-Ed Publishing

Name: .... Year: .... Date: ....

Task assessment

Activity objectives

Arts ideas: *Creates artworks to express ideas.*

Arts skills and processes: *Uses a range of visual arts skills, techniques, procedures, practices and technologies.*

Arts responses: *Uses an aesthetic understanding to acknowledge, reflect on and assess the arts.*

Arts in society: *Demonstrates an understanding of the part that the arts play in society.*

Task

The students were instructed to make a 'sun' oil pastel picture using
a range of skills, techniques, mediums and materials.

Assessment key		
✔ **yes** (has demonstrated achievement of this criterion)		
✘ **no** (has not demonstrated achievement of this criterion)		
● **inconsistent** (some evidence of achievement has been shown)		
Criteria		
The student is able to:	✔	✘ ●
participate in discussion about summer and the sun.		
demonstrate drawing strong, solid lines to make an effective resistance to dye.		
smudge consecutive circles from centre outwards using index finger.		
paint dye over oil pastel smudge drawing.		
add yellow pearl paint and craft glue with gold glitter to the picture.		
complete a reflection sheet based on his/her artwork.		
listen to and follow instructions.		
work cooperatively in an informal activity-based work environment.		

Primary art 45

R.I.C. Publications/Prim-Ed Publishing

Colourful patchwork

This lesson was inspired by the theme *Colour*. Warm and cool colours were the focus. The students chose either to colour their patchwork designs/patterns.

Two-lesson project

Discussion points

Cellophane pieces, in primary colours, can be used to demonstrate colour blending to make secondary colours.

- What is your favourite colour? (List colours on the board.)
- Do you know which colours are the primary colours? (red, blue, yellow)

  Primary colours can be mixed together to make different colours.
- Do you know which colours make green? (yellow and blue)
- Do you know which colours make purple? (red and blue)
- Do you know which colours make orange? (yellow and red)
- Which colours are cool colours? (blue, green, purple)
- Which colours are warm colours? (red, orange, yellow)
- What is patchwork? (Decorative sections of fabrics put together or overlaid to make a picture or pattern.)

Lesson two

Materials

- reflection and assessment photocopies
- lead pencil
- coloured pencils

Method

1. Students complete reflection activity.
2. Teacher completes assessment record.

Lesson one

Materials

- A3 cartridge paper
- lead pencil
- permanent black marker
- wax crayons
- oil pastels
- craft glue for mounting
- coloured card for mounting
- newspaper to protect workspace

Method

1. Following discussion about warm and cool colours, students use lead pencil to draw a patchwork design on A3 cartridge paper.
2. Trace over outline using permanent black marker.
3. Using wax crayons or oil pastels, colour design using strong, solid colour.
★ 4. Enlist adult help to mount completed artwork on coloured card.

R.I.C. Publications/Prim-Ed Publishing

Colourful patchwork

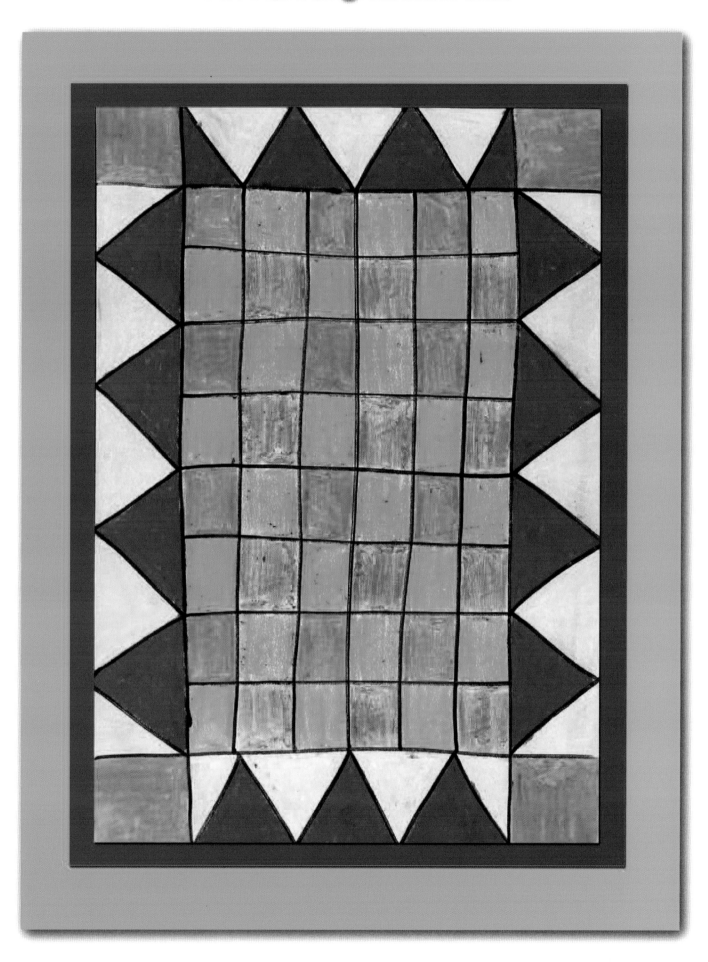

R.I.C. Publications/Prim-Ed Publishing

Colourful patchwork

Reflections

1. *Colour the techniques used to make your picture.*

colouring solid colour with wax crayons or oil pastels
painting using dye and a brush
drawing a design outline with permanent black marker
sponge painting using paint

2. *Which part of the activity did you enjoy most?*

drawing a patchwork design using lead pencil

tracing over lead pencil design using permanent black marker

colouring your design with strong, solid colour

3. *Why did you enjoy this part of the activity most?*

_____

_____

4. *What are the three primary colours?*

_____   _____   _____

5. *List three cool colours.*

_____   _____   _____

6. *List three warm colours.*

_____   _____   _____

7. *Use lead pencil to draw another patchwork design. Colour your design using pencils in warm or cool colours.*

R.I.C. Publications/Prim-Ed Publishing

Colourful patchwork
Task assessment

Activity objectives

Arts ideas: *Creates artworks to express ideas.*

Arts skills and processes: *Uses a range of visual arts skills, techniques, procedures, practices and technologies.*

Arts responses: *Uses an aesthetic understanding to acknowledge, reflect on and assess the arts.*

Arts in society: *Demonstrates an understanding of the part that the arts play in society.*

Task

The students were instructed to make a 'colourful patchwork' design using a
range of skills, techniques and materials.

Assessment key		
✔ **yes** (has demonstrated achievement of this criterion)		
✗ **no** (has not demonstrated achievement of this criterion)		
● **inconsistent** (some evidence of achievement has been shown)		
Criteria		
The student is able to:	✔	✗ ●
participate in class discussion about colours and patchwork.		
draw a patchwork design using lead pencil.		
trace over lead pencil design with a permanent black marker.		
demonstrate 'solid' colouring using wax crayons and/or oil pastels.		
complete a reflection sheet based on his/her artwork.		
listen to and follow instructions.		
work cooperatively in an informal activity-based work environment.		

Space scene

This lesson was inspired by the theme *Space*.

Three-lesson project

Discussion points

Stimulus pictures of rockets (if available) will enhance meaningful discussion responses.

- How do we travel to school? (cars, bus, bike) List responses on the board.
- If we want to travel from one side of the country to the other, how could we get there? (car, bus, train, plane)
- If we want to travel to another country, how could we get there? (plane, ship)
- If we want to travel to another planet, or the moon, how could we get there? (rocket)
- Who would travel in a rocket? (astronauts)

Lesson one

Materials

- A3 cartridge paper
- ★ craft glue (mixed in a ratio of ³/₄ glue: ¹/₄ water)
- polystyrene trays (for glue)
- dark blue tissue paper
- glue brushes
- newspaper to protect workspace
- craft glue (not diluted) for mounting
- coloured card for mounting
- cutter or scissors for trimming/neatening the edges of work in readiness for mounting

Method

1. Following discussion about space, students paint watered-down glue onto small area of A3 cartridge paper and lay a small piece of tissue paper over it. Students brush glue over it to make it smooth. (Ensure that the edges are flat.)
2. Continue overlaying torn tissue paper until all the paper is covered. Set aside to dry.
★ 3. Enlist adult help to trim and mount tissue background onto coloured card before Lesson two.

Lesson two

Materials

- mounted background
- silver metallic paper (20 cm x 15 cm)
- scrap paper (20 cm x 15 cm)
- craft glue (squeeze bottle)
- red and yellow paint (squeeze bottles or polystryrene trays and spoons)
- matchsticks
- lead pencil
- white paint

- paintbrush (fine)
- scissors
- silver glitter
- newspaper to protect workspace

Method

1. Using scrap paper, demonstrate how to make a simple paper plane.
2. Students make a paper plane/rocket of their choice using scrap paper. If they are keen to venture into different folding, this should be encouraged.
3. Copy paper folding using metallic paper.
4. Position rocket onto background.
5. Using lead pencil, trace rocket shape onto background, then set rocket aside.
★ 6. Teacher and/or enlisted adult help to squeeze or spoon small blobs of red and yellow paint at the end of rocket jets.
7. Using a matchstick, drag paint in an outward direction. (This will make a flame shape and blend the two colours to give a flame-like appearance.)
8. Using brush handle end and white paint, print the Milky Way. Set aside to dry.

Lesson three

Materials

- artwork in progress
- reflection and assessment photocopies
- gold and/or silver glitter
- craft glue
- paintbrush (fine)
- polystyrene trays (for craft glue)
- lead pencil
- coloured pencils
- glue stick
- newspaper to protect workspace

Method

1. Using glue stick, glue rocket in place on previously traced rocket shape on background.
2. Using a fine paintbrush, add craft glue lines to create the effect of motion.
3. Sprinkle with gold or silver glitter.
4. Using paintbrush handle end and craft glue, add more stars to the Milky Way and sprinkle with silver glitter. Set aside to dry.
5. Students complete reflection activity.
6. Teacher completes assessment record.

R.I.C. Publications/Prim-Ed Publishing

Space scene

Space scene

Reflections

1. Colour the mediums, materials and tools used to make your 'space scene'.

wax crayons	craft glue	permanent black marker
scrap paper	oil pastels	tissue paper
metallic paper	glitter	red, white and yellow paint
glue stick	paintbrush	scissors
matchstick	dye	craft sticks

2. Circle the part of the activity you enjoyed most.

making the tissue background

making a practice model of your rocket using scrap paper

making a folded metallic paper rocket

tracing the folded rocket shape onto the background

making flames by dragging red and yellow paint with a matchstick

printing the Milky Way background using the end of a paintbrush handle,
white paint, craft glue and silver glitter

gluing your rocket into position on your picture

enhancing your space scene with glitter highlights

3. Why did you enjoy this part of the activity most?

_____

4. What colours blended together make the colour orange?

_____ + _____ = *orange*

5. Use lead pencil to draw another picture using the paint dragging technique as a feature. Colour the picture using pencils.

Space scene
Task assessment

Activity objectives

Arts ideas: *Creates artworks to express ideas.*

Arts skills and processes: *Uses a range of visual arts skills, techniques, procedures, practices and technologies.*

Arts responses: *Uses an aesthetic understanding to acknowledge, reflect on and assess the arts.*

Arts in society: *Demonstrates an understanding of the part that the arts play in society.*

Task

The students were instructed to make a 'space' picture using a range of skills, techniques, mediums and materials.

Assessment key			
✔ **yes** *(has demonstrated achievement of this criterion)*			
✗ **no** *(has not demonstrated achievement of this criterion)*			
● **inconsistent** *(some evidence of achievement has been shown)*			
Criteria			
The student is able to:	✔	✗	●
participate in class discussion about space travel.			
make a tissue background.			
practise making a folded rocket using scrap paper.			
make a folded rocket shape using metallic paper.			
trace a folded rocket shape onto background using lead pencil.			
demonstrate paint dragging technique using a matchstick.			
demonstrate dot printing using paint and the end of a paintbrush handle.			
demonstrate dot printing using craft glue, and the end of a paintbrush handle, then sprinkling with silver glitter.			
glue rocket into position.			
add glitter highlights.			
complete a reflection sheet based on his/her artwork.			
listen to and follow instructions.			
work cooperatively in an informal activity-based work environment.			

Shape aliens

This project was inspired by the maths strand *Shape and space*. (Topic: *Shapes – squares, triangles, rectangles, circles, pentagons and hexagons*) This project followed an intensive series of lessons covering the features and characteristics of the shapes listed.

Two-lesson project

Discussion points

- What is an alien? (Someone born in another country and has not yet gained citizenship. In terms of 'space' – a being who is not naturally present on Earth.)
- What might an alien from space look like? (Take suggestions from students and draw their ideas on a board.)
- If an alien was made from 2-D shapes, what might he/she/it look like? What shapes would you use? (square, rectangle, triangle, rhombus, pentagon, hexagon etc.) Draw these shapes on the board. Discuss features: number of sides and number of corners etc.

Lesson one

Materials

- *A3 coloured card*
- *A4 photocopy paper*
- *bottle lids (for tracing circles)*
- *ruler*
- *coloured paper*
- *metallic paper (optional)*
- *scissors*
- *glue stick*
- *lead pencil*
- *newspaper to protect workspace*
- *coloured card for mounting*
- *craft glue for mounting*

Method

1. Following discussion about shapes and the features of each, students use a lead pencil to draw an alien on A4 paper, incorporating the shapes discussed. (A plan.)
2. Commence drawing and tracing shapes onto the back of coloured and metallic paper, following the drawn plan. (Emphasise using a ruler to make straight edges.)
3. Cut out the shapes.
4. Arrange shapes onto coloured card to make an alien.
5. Using glue stick, glue shapes into position.
★ 6. Enlist adult help to mount 'shape alien' pictures.

Lesson two

Materials

- *reflection and assessment photocopies*
- *lead pencil*
- *coloured pencils*

Method

1. Students complete reflection activity.
2. Teacher completes assessment record.

Shape aliens

R.I.C. Publications/Prim-Ed Publishing

Shape aliens

Reflections

1. *Colour the mediums, materials and tools used to make your 'shape alien'.*

wax crayons	craft glue	coloured paper	scissors
ruler	container lid	A4 paper	lead pencil
glue stick	A3 coloured card	circles to trace	sponges

2. *Circle the part of the activity you enjoyed most.*

drawing the plan for your 'shape alien'

drawing and tracing the shapes on the back of the coloured paper

cutting out the coloured paper shapes

arranging the shapes into position to make a 'shape alien'

gluing the shapes into position

3. *List the number of sides the following shapes have.*

triangle _____   circle _____

pentagon _____   square _____

rectangle _____   hexagon _____

4. *With a lead pencil, draw a picture using all of the shapes listed above. Colour the picture with pencils.*

R.I.C. Publications/Prim-Ed Publishing

Shape aliens
Task assessment

Activity objectives

Arts ideas: *Creates artworks to express ideas.*

Arts skills and processes: *Uses a range of visual arts skills, techniques, procedures, practices and technologies.*

Arts responses: *Uses an aesthetic understanding to acknowledge, reflect on and assess the arts.*

Arts in society: *Demonstrates an understanding of the part that the arts play in society.*

Task

The students were instructed to make a picture of a 'shape alien' using
a range of skills, techniques, mediums and materials.

Assessment key			
✔ **yes** *(has demonstrated achievement of this criterion)*			
✗ **no** *(has not demonstrated achievement of this criterion)*			
● **inconsistent** *(some evidence of achievement has been shown)*			
Criteria			
The student is able to:	✔	✗	●
participate in class discussion about 'shapes and aliens'.			
draw a plan of an alien made from shapes.			
draw, trace and rule shapes onto the back of coloured paper.			
cut out coloured paper shapes.			
arrange shapes and glue into position using glue stick.			
complete a reflection sheet based on his/her artwork.			
listen to and follow instructions.			
work cooperatively in an informal activity-based work environment.			

Primary art **57**

Rapunzel

This activity was inspired by the theme *Fairytales*. A story map was completed and the children were instructed to make a scene of Rapunzel in the tower.

Three-lesson project

Discussion points

- Read the children any version of the fairytale, *Rapunzel*.
- List the sequence of events in the story in point form on the board.
- What did you like about the character, Rapunzel? (kind, sweet etc.)
- What did you like about the character, the prince. (noble, kind, doing what was right etc.)
- Would the prince be a good citizen? Why? (He would be helpful and help others in need.)
- How did Rapunzel help the prince to climb the tower? (letting down her beautiful hair)
- When making a picture of this scene from the story, what else could you include? (bushes, rocks, a tree etc.)

Lesson one

Materials

- A3 cartridge paper
- permanent black marker
- wax crayons
- oil pastels
- Edicol™ or vegetable dye (blue)
- paintbrush (medium)
- acrylic paint (brown and green)
- sponges (cut to size to print bricks on the tower)
- polystyrene trays (for paint)
- scissors
- lead pencil
- newspaper to protect workspace
- coloured card for mounting
- craft glue for mounting

Method

1. Following story and related discussion, students use permanent black marker to draw a castle-like tower with a large window at the top (as shown in example).
2. Draw Rapunzel looking out of the window and the prince at the bottom of the tower.
3. Colour Rapunzel and the prince, using wax crayons and/or oil pastels, in strong, solid colour.
4. Locate a rough, textured area (e.g. concrete, brick paving).
5. Lightly rub brown crayon over textured surface to create an effective texture for the wall of the tower. Do the same using green wax crayon, to make a textured landscape at the bottom of and around the tower.

6. Using a rectangular block sponge and brown paint, print brick shapes using 'pat and lift' technique. Emphasise 'pat and lift' (no dragging).
7. Using dye and medium brush, paint sky.
8. Using sponge and green paint, create bushes and remaining landscape. Set aside to dry.
★ 9. Enlist adult help to mount pictures before Lesson two.

Lesson two

Materials

- artwork in progress
- yellow wool
★ - thick cardboard cut to size (20 cm x 10 cm)
- ribbon, cord, raffia to tie braid
- hot glue gun
- scissors

Method

1. Wind wool around the length of the cardboard 21 times.
2. Use another length of wool to tie the middle.
3. Using scissors, cut through all strands about one-third of the way down one side.
★ 4. In partners, students braid the longest lengths. There should be about seven strands in each section. Tie braid with cord or ribbon.
★ 5. Enlist adult helper to hot glue braid into position, trimming top neatly (as shown in example).

Lesson three

Materials

- reflection and assessment photocopies
- lead pencil
- coloured pencils

Method

1. Students complete reflection activity.
2. Teacher completes assessment record.

Rapunzel

R.I.C. Publications/Prim-Ed Publishing

Rapunzel

Reflections

1. *Circle the part of the activity you enjoyed most.*

drawing the picture with permanent black marker

colouring the picture with wax crayons and oil pastels

making texture rubbings with wax crayons

painting with dye

sponge painting with paint

2. *Why did you enjoy this part of the activity most?*

_____

_____

3. *Which part of the story of Rapunzel did you enjoy most? Why?*

_____

_____

4. *List five materials, mediums or tools you used to make your 'Rapunzel' picture.*

_____

_____

5. *Use lead pencil to draw your favourite part of the story. Colour your picture with pencils.*

Rapunzel

Task assessment

Activity objectives

Arts ideas: *Creates artworks to express ideas.*

Arts skills and processes: *Uses a range of visual arts skills, techniques, procedures, practices and technologies.*

Arts responses: *Uses an aesthetic understanding to acknowledge, reflect on and assess the arts.*

Arts in society: *Demonstrates an understanding of the part that the arts play in society.*

Task

The students were instructed to make a 'Rapunzel' picture using a
range of skills, techniques, mediums and materials.

Assessment key		
✔ **yes** *(has demonstrated achievement of this criterion)*		
✗ **no** *(has not demonstrated achievement of this criterion)*		
● **inconsistent** *(some evidence of achievement has been shown)*		
Criteria		
The student is able to:	✔	✗ ●
listen to the story Rapunzel.		
participate in class discussion about Rapunzel.		
draw a scene from Rapunzel*: the tower, Rapunzel and the prince.*		
use wax crayons and/or oil pastels to colour Rapunzel and the prince.		
make a texture rubbing using wax crayon.		
paint with dye to colour the sky and landscape.		
sponge paint brick shapes onto the tower.		
sponge paint bushes and landscape.		
make hair by winding wool around prepared card.		
braid wool.		
complete a reflection sheet based on his/her artwork.		
listen to and follow instructions.		
work cooperatively in an informal activity-based work environment.		

Primary art **61**

Beach babes

This project was inspired by the theme *Seasons* (Topic: *Summer*). Sun safety was incorporated into the discussion relating to 'good health practices'.

Three-lesson project

Discussion points

- Have you ever been swimming at the beach?
- What do you do when you get out of the water? (dry off)
- How do we dry off? (use a towel, lie in the sun for a short time)
- How do you stand, sit or lie on a surfboard?
- What should we wear while we are swimming? (sun protective clothing, sunscreen and a hat etc.)
- Why shouldn't we stay in the sun for very long? (sun danger, harmful nature of UV rays etc.)
- What is the most effective sun protection factor in sun screens? (SPF 30)
- How often should we reapply sunscreen? (Read the instructions, answers vary according to conditions.)

Lesson one

Materials

- A3 cartridge paper (loosely fold it into thirds) (portrait)
- permanent black markers
- wax crayons
- oil pastels
- newspaper to protect workspace

Method

1. Following discussion, distribute paper.
2. Students use a permanent black marker to complete a step-by-step drawing of themselves lying on a brightly coloured/patterned beach towel (see illustration).
3. Colour child with wax crayons and/or oil pastels. Emphasise the importance of 'solid' colour.

Lesson two

Materials

- artwork in progress
- Edicol™ vegetable dye (yellow)
- wax crayons
- oil pastels
- paintbrush (medium)
- lead pencil
- craft glue for mounting
- coloured card for mounting
- newspaper to protect workspace

Method

1. If necessary, complete colouring started in Lesson one.
2. Locate a rough surface and, using a yellow wax crayon, rub over to form a grainy texture to represent the sand.
3. Paint background using watery yellow dye.
★ 4. Enlist adult helper to mount pictures onto coloured card.

Lesson three

Materials

- reflection and assessment photocopies
- lead pencil
- coloured pencils

Method

1. Students complete reflection activity.
2. Teacher completes assessment record.

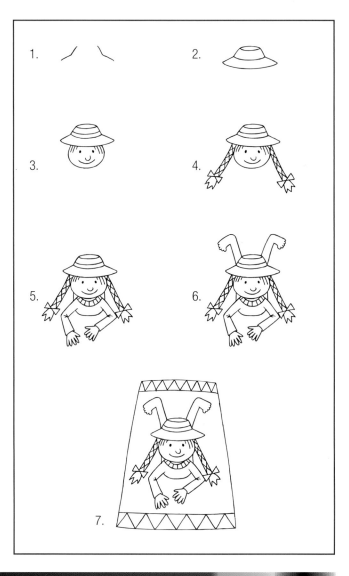

R.I.C. Publications/Prim-Ed Publishing

Beach babes

R.I.C. Publications/Prim-Ed Publishing

Beach babes

Reflections

1. Colour the mediums, materials and tools you used to make your picture.

wax crayons	dye	permanent black marker
tissue paper	glitter	medium paintbrush
oil pastels	metallic paper	lead pencil
craft sticks	cartridge paper	wool

2. Circle the part of the activity you enjoyed most.

drawing yourself lying on a beach towel

designing a pattern on your beach towel

colouring with oil pastels and/or wax crayons

texture rubbing using a wax crayon

painting background with dye

3. Tick the items that may help to protect you from the sun.

sunscreen SPF 30	hand lotion	lip balm SPF 30
beach umbrella	sunglasses	hat
rash shirt	long sleeved T-shirt	beach ball
surfboard	long trousers	sandals

4. Why is it important to stay out of the sun as much as possible?

_____

_____

_____

_____

_____

_____

5. Draw yourself wearing sun protective clothing.

R.I.C. Publications/Prim-Ed Publishing

Beach babes
Task assessment

Activity objectives

Arts ideas: *Creates artworks to express ideas.*

Arts skills and processes: *Uses a range of visual arts skills, techniques, procedures, practices and technologies.*

Arts responses: *Uses an aesthetic understanding to acknowledge, reflect on and assess the arts.*

Arts in society: *Demonstrates an understanding of the part that the arts play in society.*

Task

The students were instructed to make a picture of themselves lying on a beach towel using a 'step-by-step' process and a range of colouring mediums.

Assessment key			
✔ **yes** *(has demonstrated achievement of this criterion)*			
✘ **no** *(has not demonstrated achievement of this criterion)*			
● **inconsistent** *(some evidence of achievement has been shown)*			
Criteria			
The student is able to:	✔	✘	●
participate in discussion about the beach and sun safety.			
use permanent black marker to complete a step-by-step drawing of himself/ herself lying on a patterned beach towel.			
colour himself/herself and towel using wax crayons and/or oil pastels.			
complete a texture rubbing using wax crayon and a rough surface.			
paint over wax texture rubbing using dye.			
complete a reflection sheet based on his/her artwork.			
listen to and follow instructions.			
work cooperatively in an informal activity-based work environment.			

Autumn leaves repetitive drawing collage

This lesson can be related to any theme; The guidelines change according to the topic. The theme for the example shown was *The seasons*, (Topic: *autumn*).

Two-lesson project

Discussion point

A collection of leaves with varied shapes is a useful resource to inspire children to create the initial drawing. The leaves may be collected by the teacher or the students.

- What are the seasons? (summer, autumn, winter, spring)
- What sort of weather do we experience in:

  summer? - warm, hot

  autumn? - warm, cool

  winter? - cool, cold

  spring? - cool, warm
- During autumn, what happens to the leaves of many trees? (They change colour from green to various shades of warm colours and fall off the trees.)
- Do you know the name for trees which lose their leaves in autumn? (deciduous)
- What happens to these trees as winter changes to spring? (new leaf growth)
- What are warm/autumn colours? (yellows, oranges, reds, browns)

Lesson one

Materials
- A3 cartridge paper
- A5 photocopy paper
- ★ leaf-shaped template (optional) (page 126)
- ★ collection of leaves with varied shapes (optional)
- lead pencil
- permanent black marker
- newspaper to protect workspace

Method
1. Following discussion about 'the seasons' and 'autumn', the students select a leaf shape to draw as the basis of their collage. (You may decide to use the template provided in the resources.)
2. Using lead pencil, draw a leaf shape onto A5 paper.
3. Trace over pencil outline using permanent black marker.
4. Using lead pencil, trace leaf design onto A3 cartridge paper. Repeat tracing, demonstrating depth by overlapping tracings. Emphasise that we only draw what we can see if another leaf is overlapping our initial drawing. (Draw at least five tracings.)
5. Trace over lead pencil lines using permanent black marker.

Lesson two

Materials
- artwork in progress
- wax crayons (warm colours)
- Edicol™ or vegetable dye (warm colours)
- paintbrush (medium)
- newspaper to protect workspace
- coloured card for mounting
- craft glue for mounting
- reflection and assessment photocopies
- lead pencil
- coloured pencils

Method
1. Using wax crayons, colour leaf tracings with warm/autumn colours.
2. Locate a rough textured surface (concrete, brick paving) and, using wax crayon, rub around coloured leaves.
3. Paint over texture rubbing with dye, using another warm colour. Set aside to dry.
4. Students complete reflection activity.
5. Teacher completes assessment record.
★ 6. Enlist adult help to mount pictures onto coloured card.

R.I.C. Publications/Prim-Ed Publishing

Autumn leaves repetitive drawing collage

R.I.C. Publications/Prim-Ed Publishing

Autumn leaves repetitive drawing collage

Reflections

1. What are the four seasons?

   _____   _____

   _____   _____

2. Circle the part of this activity you enjoyed the most.

   drawing/tracing a leaf shape with lead pencil

   going over the leaf shape with a permanent black marker

   tracing the leaf shape many times using a lead pencil

   tracing over lead pencil lines with permanent black marker

   colouring the drawn collage with wax crayons

   making a texture rubbing background using wax crayon

   painting dye over the texture rubbing

3. Which warm colours did you use?

   _____

4. What happens to a deciduous tree in autumn?

   _____

5. Colour the word(s) which could describe the weather in autumn.

hot	freezing	cool	warm

6. Use lead pencil to draw yourself playing in the leaves during autumn.

   Colour your picture with warm-coloured pencils.

R.I.C. Publications/Prim-Ed Publishing

Autumn leaves repetitive drawing collage
Task assessment

Activity objectives

Arts ideas: *Creates artworks to express ideas.*

Arts skills and processes: *Uses a range of visual arts skills, techniques, procedures, practices and technologies.*

Arts responses: *Uses an aesthetic understanding to acknowledge, reflect on and assess the arts.*

Arts in society: *Demonstrates an understanding of the part that the arts play in society.*

Task

The students were instructed to make a 'leaf drawing collage' using a
range of skills, techniques, mediums and materials.

Assessment key			
✔ **yes** *(has demonstrated achievement of this criterion)*			
✗ **no** *(has not demonstrated achievement of this criterion)*			
● **inconsistent** *(some evidence of achievement has been shown)*			
Criteria			
The student is able to:	✔	✗	●
participate in discussion about the seasons and autumn.			
draw/trace a picture of a leaf.			
trace leaf shape at least five times onto A3 cartridge paper to form a repetitive drawing collage.			
trace over lead pencil lines using permanent black marker.			
demonstrate solid colouring using warm-coloured wax crayons.			
make a wax crayon texture rubbing.			
paint dye over wax crayon texture rubbing.			
complete a reflection sheet based on his/her artwork.			
listen to and follow instructions.			
work cooperatively in an informal activity-based work environment.			

Rock and roll tie

This project was inspired by the music theme *Rock'n'roll*. Music from many eras can be the focus for 'creative' and 'glitzy' artwork. If there is a music specialist in your teaching team, it is a great opportunity to work together on this theme. Alternatively, the children can design a tie for any occasion; e.g. for Dad for his birthday. Children enjoy thinking of themselves as fashion designers and can design an appropriate tie for a chosen person. The tie in the example incorporates summer storms, fishing, music and gardens.

Two-lesson project

Discussion points

Album covers are a great resource, along with popular music played by the parents of the children, as this is what they will hear at home.

- What is rock music? (music with a strong rhythm, very appropriate to dancing)
- Why do people like rock music? (can dance to it, sing along with it, listen to it for pleasure)
- What is a rock star? (someone who plays rock music which is popular)
- What does a rock star do? (entertains people)
- Who is your favourite rock star? (List the stars on the board.)
- What does a rock star wear to attract attention? (List items of clothing on the board, especially gear typically worn by a star performing. Album covers may have pictures of stars in glitzy gear; e.g. Elvis Presley.)
- If you were a rock star, what kind of clothing would you wear?
- What kind of hairstyle would you have?
- We are going to design a tie for a rock star to wear. Think about the rock star the tie is for. What things other than music might he/she be interested in?
- Discuss what pursuits the person may have enjoyed in the example shown.

Method

1. Following discussion about rock stars and what they wear while entertaining, demonstrate how to draw a range of patterns and pictures using lead pencil on the tie shape. Emphasise that the clothes and accessories should grab attention. A fashion designer would create clothes specifically for the star. Suggest some techniques to add colour to the tie; e.g. segments of dye, wax crayons and/or pastels, and glitter (if available). Students should have a mental image of their design.
2. Using lead pencil, draw tie design onto tie proforma.
3. Trace over pencil lines with permanent black marker.
4. Colour designs using available resources (as listed above.) Set aside to dry if required.
5. When dry, cut out tie.
6. Paint areas requiring glitter enhancement with craft glue.
★ 7. Sprinkle with glitter. Set adsie to dry. Ties may be mounted or pegged on a line to display.

Lesson two

Materials

- *reflection and assessment photocopies*
- *lead pencil*
- *coloured pencils*

Method

1. Students complete reflection activity.
2. Teacher completes assessment record.

Lesson one

Materials

★ - *photocopy of tie shape on cartridge paper (see page 126)*
- *paintbrushes (medium and fine)*
- *lead pencil*
- *permanent black markers*
- *wax crayons and/or oil pastels*
- *Edicol™ or vegetable dye*
- *glitter*
- *craft glue (squeeze bottle)*
- *polystyrene trays (for craft glue)*
- *scissors*
- *glue stick*
- *newspaper to protect workspace*

Rock and roll tie

Rock and roll tie

Reflections

1. Circle the mediums, materials and tools used to make your 'rock and roll' tie.

wax crayons	dye	glitter
craft glue	paint	scissors
paintbrush	oil pastels	lead pencil
tissue paper	permanent black marker	wool

2. Which part of this activity did you enjoy the most? Give a reason for your answer.

_____

_____

_____

3. Design a 'rock and roll' tie for your dad to wear. Remember to include things that your dad enjoys. Use pencils to add colour to your picture.

What do your designs tell us about your dad?

_____

_____

_____

_____

_____

_____

_____

_____

_____

_____

_____

R.I.C. Publications/Prim-Ed Publishing

Rock and roll tie
Task assessment

Activity objectives

Arts ideas: *Creates artworks to express ideas.*

Arts skills and processes: *Uses a range of visual arts skills, techniques, procedures, practices and technologies.*

Arts responses: *Uses an aesthetic understanding to acknowledge, reflect on and assess the arts.*

Arts in society: *Demonstrates an understanding of the part that the arts play in society.*

Task

The students were instructed to make a 'rock star tie' picture using a range of skills, techniques, mediums and materials.

Assessment key			
✔ **yes** *(has demonstrated achievement of this criterion)*			
✘ **no** *(has not demonstrated achievement of this criterion)*			
● **inconsistent** *(some evidence of achievement has been shown)*			
Criteria			
The student is able to:	✔	✘	●
participate in discussion about rock stars, music and fashion design.			
draw designs onto tie proforma using lead pencil.			
trace over pencil lines using permanent black marker.			
demonstrate strong, solid colouring using wax crayons and/or oil pastels.			
paint dye around wax crayon and oil pastel colouring.			
paint craft glue onto selected sections of design to add glitter enhancement.			
complete a reflection sheet based on his/her artwork.			
listen to and follow instructions.			
work cooperatively in an informal activity-based work environment.			

Primary art **73**

Look what I can see through the gate!

This project may be related to any topic; hence, there are numerous scenes that can go behind the 'gate'. The scene in the example is 'The beach'.

Three-lesson project

Discussion points

The discussion points for this art piece will be wide and varied, depending on the theme/topic. Discussion questions for the example relate to 'my favourite place'.

- Where is your favourite place? Prompt ideas; for example: To go for holidays? To read a book? To play with your friends? Places may also relate to seasons. (Answers will vary according to personal likes.)
- Prompt thoughtful planning.
- If you love to go to the beach, what might be in your beach scene? (the sea, sandcastle, shells, boats, beach umbrellas, bodyboards, people etc.)

Lesson one

Materials

- craft sticks
- craft glue (squeeze bottle)
- glue brushes
- polystyrene meat trays on which to construct the gate
- A5 photocopy paper
- lead pencil/eraser
- newspaper to protect workspace

Method

1. Following discussion, make the gate by lying three craft sticks horizontally on the tray.
2. Place the remaining craft sticks on top until satisfied with positioning.
3. Using brushes and craft glue, attach one craft stick in position at a time. Set aside to dry.
4. Using lead pencil, draw/sketch a plan of the basic outline of your favourite scene onto A5 photocopy paper.

Lesson two

Materials

- artwork in progress
★ - cartridge paper cut to size (14 cm x 18 cm)
- polystyrene trays (for paint)
- paint
- small block sponges
- small brushes
- scrap coloured paper to add extras to the picture; e.g. cellophane for water
- small shells (if available)
- glue stick

- craft glue (squeeze bottle)
- lead pencil
- wax crayons
- oil pastels
- Edicol™ or vegetable dye
- newspaper to protect workspace

Method

1. Copy basic plan onto cartridge paper.
2. Using available mediums and resources, add detail and colour to picture. Students are encouraged to use a range of mediums and choose from their repertoire of previously tried skills (see example).

Example using specified equipment (Lesson two method)

1. Using lead pencil, draw detail onto drawing.
2. Colour people and objects using wax crayons and oil pastels.
3. Locate a rough textured surface and, using yellow wax crayon, make a texture rubbing to give beach sand a gritty appearance.
4. Paint over wax texture rubbing with yellow dye.
5. Paint background with blue dye. Set aside to dry.

Lesson three

Materials

- artwork in progress
- glue stick
- craft glue
- polystyrene trays (for craft glue)
- glitter (optional)
- strong, clear tape
- newspaper to protect workspace
- reflection and assessment photocopies
- lead pencil
- coloured pencils
- fine black marker
★ - thick cardboard cut to size (14 cm x 18 cm)

Method

1. Using fine black marker, trace over pencil lines to enhance detail.
2. Using glue stick, glue picture to thick cardboard.
★ 3. Enlist adult help to assist children to tape gate to picture. (Artwork will become freestanding.)
4. Using craft glue, paint area for glitter highlights.
5. Sprinkle with glitter.
6. Students complete reflection activity.
7. Teacher completes assessment record.

Look what I can see through the gate!

R.I.C. Publications/Prim-Ed Publishing

Look what I can see through the gate!

Reflections

1. What 'favourite place' did you choose for your picture?

   _____

2. Circle the part of the activity you enjoyed the most.

   making the gate using craft sticks and craft glue

   drawing the outline/plan

   drawing the picture onto cartridge paper

   choosing mediums, materials and tools to make your picture

   making your picture

3. Colour the mediums, materials and tools used to make your picture.

paint	sponges	paintbrush
dye	tissue paper	craft glue
glue stick	wax crayons	oil pastels
lead pencil	cellophane	scissors
glitter	permanent black marker	fine black marker

4. Which part of the activity did you enjoy the most?
   Give a reason for your answer.

   _____

   _____

5. Use lead pencil to draw another scene you would like to find behind your
   gate. Colour your picture with pencils.

R.I.C. Publications/Prim-Ed Publishing

Look what I can see through the gate!

Task assessment

Activity objectives

Arts ideas: *Creates artworks to express ideas.*

Arts skills and processes: *Uses a range of visual arts skills, techniques, procedures, practices and technologies.*

Arts responses: *Uses an aesthetic understanding to acknowledge, reflect on and assess the arts.*

Arts in society: *Demonstrates an understanding of the part that the arts play in society.*

Task

The students were instructed to make a 'picket gate' and a 'favourite place' scene using a range of skills, techniques, mediums and materials.

Assessment key			
✔ **yes** (has demonstrated achievement of this criterion)			
✘ **no** (has not demonstrated achievement of this criterion)			
● **inconsistent** (some evidence of achievement has been shown)			
Criteria			
The student is able to:	✔	✘	●
participate in discussion about 'favourite places'.			
make a miniature gate using craft sticks and craft glue.			
draw a plan of his/her favourite place.			
create a 'favourite place' picture using a range of materials and mediums.			
complete a reflection sheet based on his/her artwork.			
listen to and follow instructions.			
work cooperatively in an informal activity-based work environment.			

Primary art 77

Birds of peacefulness

This lesson was inspired by the health area **Values**—the topic was **Peacefulness**; being calm and having time for themselves. Birds of peace were discussed and the idea of 'birds of peacefulness' introduced.

Two-lesson project

Discussion points

- What does the word 'peaceful' mean? (quiet, calm, serene)
- Do you ever have peaceful times? When?
- Why do we need peaceful times? (We lead very busy lives and sometimes we need to have time to stop and relax, think and enjoy our own company.)
- What are birds of peace? (white doves are a symbol of peace)
- Peacefulness is something everyone should experience, if not all the time, at least some time during each day. (The birds we are making are a reminder for us to take time out for ourselves.)

Lesson one

Materials

- ★ *prepared template of basic bird shape (page 127)*
- *firm cardboard (such as a cereal box)*
- ★ *coloured card (25 cm x 25 cm)*
- ★ *coloured paper (cut into strips 1.5 cm wide)*
- *10 mm goggle eye*
- *small coin*
- *scissors*
- *stapler*
- *glue stick*
- *lead pencil*
- *ribbon or fishing line*
- *newspaper to protect workspace*
- *craft glue (squeeze bottle)*

Method

1. Following discussion about the virtue 'peacefulness', using lead pencil, students trace bird-shaped template onto firm cardboard.
2. Cut out traced bird shape.
3. Choose coloured paper strips and cut into squares.
4. Using glue stick, glue coloured paper squares, as a paper mosaic, onto bird shape. Emphasise gluing all edges down flat.
5. When first side is completely covered with paper mosaic, turn bird over and, using scissors, trim around bird shape.
6. Colour the other side of the bird using paper mosaic.
7. Using scissors, trim around the bird shape again.
8. Using lead pencil, trace around a coin onto the back of coloured paper twice.
9. Cut around traced circles and, using glue stick, glue circles onto bird as eye background.

10. Fan fold square coloured card (approximately 2 cm wide folds).
★11. Enlist adult help to cut slit in bird and insert wing. Staple across the slit twice to keep wings in place.
12. Thread ribbon or fishing line through gap under staple and tie securely.
13. Using craft glue, attach eye into position. Set aside to dry. To display 'birds of peacefulness' hang from indoor tree or dry branches in a pot.

Lesson two

Materials

- *reflection and assessment photocopies*
- *lead pencil*
- *coloured pencils*

Method

1. Students complete reflection activity.
2. Teacher completes assessment record.

R.I.C. Publications/Prim-Ed Publishing

R.I.C. Publications/Prim-Ed Publishing

Birds of peacefulness

Reflections

1. Colour the mediums, materials and tools you used to make your bird.

wax crayons	glue stick
coloured paper	scissors
lead pencil	cardboard
bird-shaped template	coloured pencils
goggle eye	craft glue

2. Which part of this activity did you enjoy most? Give a reason for your answer.

_____

_____

3. Why is it important to have a peaceful time each day? _____

_____

4. When do you have a peaceful time? _____

_____

5. Do you enjoy having peaceful time? | Yes | No |

Why?/Why not? _____

_____

6. Use lead pencil to draw another living thing which could represent 'peacefulness'. Colour your drawing with pencils.

Birds of peacefulness
Task assessment

Activity objectives

Arts ideas: *Creates artworks to express ideas.*

Arts skills and processes: *Uses a range of visual arts skills, techniques, procedures, practices and technologies.*

Arts responses: *Uses an aesthetic understanding to acknowledge, reflect on and assess the arts.*

Arts in society: *Demonstrates an understanding of the part that the arts play in society.*

Task

The students were instructed to make a 3-D bird of peacefulness using a
range of skills, techniques, mediums and materials.

Assessment key			
✔ **yes** (has demonstrated achievement of this criterion)			
✗ **no** (has not demonstrated achievement of this criterion)			
● **inconsistent** (some evidence of achievement has been shown)			
Criteria			
The student is able to:	✔	✗	●
participate in class discussion about peacefulness and time out.			
trace a prepared bird-shaped template.			
cut out tracing.			
colour bird shape using paper mosaic technique.			
make an eye by tracing, cutting and gluing a circle shape.			
fan fold coloured cardboard or paper square.			
complete a reflection sheet based on his/her artwork.			
listen to and follow instructions.			
work cooperatively in an informal activity-based work environment.			

Crazy colour jigsaw

This project is quick and effective and requires very little preparation. Children love to have the freedom of drawing anything they choose and embrace the idea of making a puzzle for others to complete.

Two-lesson project

Discussion points

- What is a jigsaw puzzle? (a picture cut into sections; the challenge is to arrange the pieces in the correct position to form the picture)
- Why do people do jigsaws? (to relax, as a challenge, rather than watching television etc.)
- Students have the opportunity to draw anything they choose for their jigsaw picture. They will draw their picture with lead pencil and trace over the lines with permanent black marker. What would they like to draw? Make a list of suggestions from the students on the board. These will be wide and varied.
- Who would you like to do your jigsaw? (brother, sister, younger children in the school etc.)

Lesson one

Materials

- A4 cartridge paper
- lead pencil
- permanent black marker
- wax crayons
- newspaper to protect workspace
- card for mounting
- Snap lock™ plastic bags (to keep puzzles in order)
- glue stick
- scissors

Method

1. Following discussion about 'free choice' drawing and jigsaws, students use lead pencil to draw a picture.
2. Trace over pencil lines with permanent black marker.
3. Using glue stick, cover the entire back of the drawn picture with glue.
4. Glue picture onto card.
5. Turn work over and, using lead pencil, draw sections on the card to make jigsaw pieces.
6. Cut out jigsaw pieces.
7. Shuffle pieces and turn them upside down.
8. Colour picture, one piece at a time, using wax crayons. Avoid using the same colours for each part of the picture. (This will create 'crazy colours'.) Emphasise strong, solid colour. (No white showing.)

Lesson two

Materials

- reflection and assessment photocopies
- coloured pencils
- lead pencil

Method

1. Students complete reflection activity.
2. Teacher completes assessment record.

Crazy colour jigsaw

R.I.C. Publications/Prim-Ed Publishing

Crazy colour jigsaw

Reflections

1. *Circle the part of the activity you enjoyed the most.*

drawing the picture for your 'crazy colours jigsaw'

tracing your picture with permanent black marker

gluing your picture onto card

cutting out your jigsaw pieces

drawing the sections for the jigsaw pieces

colouring the jigsaw pieces using wax crayons

making the jigsaw when it was finished

2. *Why did you enjoy this part of the activity?*

_____

3. *Who would you like to make your jigsaw puzzle? Give a reason for your answer.*

_____

_____

4. *Tick the reasons why people might like to do jigsaw puzzles.*

to increase their workload ☐

to enjoy the challenge of completing a puzzle ☐

to have a rest from television ☐

to relax ☐

5. *Use lead pencil to draw another picture for a jigsaw puzzle. Colour your picture with pencils.*

R.I.C. Publications/Prim-Ed Publishing

Crazy colour jigsaw
Task assessment

Activity objectives
Arts ideas: *Creates artworks to express ideas.*
Arts skills and processes: *Uses a range of visual arts skills, techniques, procedures, practices and technologies.*
Arts responses: *Uses an aesthetic understanding to acknowledge, reflect on and assess the arts.*
Arts in society: *Demonstrates an understanding of the part that the arts play in society.*

Task
The students were instructed to make a self-drawn and coloured 'jigsaw' using a range of techniques and materials.

Assessment key			
✔ **yes** (has demonstrated achievement of this criterion)			
✗ **no** (has not demonstrated achievement of this criterion)			
● **inconsistent** (some evidence of achievement has been shown)			
Criteria			
The student is able to:	✔	✗	●
participate in discussion about jigsaw puzzles and free-choice drawing.			
draw a picture of his/her choice using lead pencil.			
trace over lead pencil lines using permanent black marker.			
glue picture onto card using glue stick.			
using lead pencil, draw puzzle sections onto the back of mounted picture.			
cut out puzzle pieces.			
demonstrate solid colouring using wax crayons.			
make the jigsaw when completed.			
complete a reflection sheet based on his/her artwork.			
listen to and follow instructions.			
work cooperatively in an informal activity-based work environment.			

Primary art **85**

Giant butterfly

This art lesson was inspired by the theme *Insects*. Stimulus photos of insects will enhance discussion.

Three-lesson project

Discussion points

- **What is an insect?** (a small invertebrate with three body parts, 3 pairs of legs and usually 2 pairs of wings)
- **What insects do you know?** (bee, grasshopper, cricket, mosquito, butterfly etc.)
- **Where have you seen a butterfly?** (Most answers will relate to gardens.)
- **What have you noticed about the wings of a butterfly?** (They are bright and colourful and are the same on either side [symmetrical].)
- **What does 'symmetrical' mean?** (even, the same on either side of a central line/point)
- **What colour are butterflies?** (all colours)

Lesson one

Materials

- A3 cartridge paper
- paint (variety of colours)
- paintbrushes (medium)
- sponges (small blocks)
- polystyrene trays (for paint)
- lead pencil
- coloured card for mounting
- craft glue for mounting
- newspaper to protect workspace

Method

1. Following discussion about insects, use paint and brush to complete part of a flower bloom, stem and leaves on A3 paper.
2. Carefully sponge paint background. Set aside to dry.
★ 3. Enlist adult help to mount work onto coloured card before Lesson two.

Lesson two

Materials

- *artwork in progress*
- *wrapping paper (30 cm x 20 cm)*
★ - *prepared butterfly shape template (page 128)*
- *sparkling pipe-cleaner (one per child)*
- *lead pencil*
- *hot glue gun*
- *newspaper to protect workspace*
- *scissors*
- *oil pastel (black)*

Method

1. Using lead pencil, trace prepared template onto the back of wrapping paper.
2. Using scissors, cut along traced lines.
3. Fan fold using small folds (as shown in example).
4. Fasten with a pipe-cleaner in the middle by twisting pipe-cleaner at the back.
5. Bring both pipe-cleaner ends to the head side of the butterfly. Turn ends up to form antennae.
6. Using black oil pastel, draw body of butterfly onto background.
★ 7. Adult to assist hot gluing butterfly into place over body shape, spreading wings accordingly.

Lesson three

Materials

- *reflection and assessment photocopies*
- *lead pencil*
- *coloured pencils*

Method

1. Students complete reflection activity.
2. Teacher completes assessment record.

R.I.C. Publications/Prim-Ed Publishing

Giant butterfly

R.I.C. Publications/Prim-Ed Publishing

Giant butterfly

Reflections

1. Colour the materials, mediums and tools used to make your picture.

wrapping paper	lead pencil	paint
wax crayons	dye	paintbrush
sparkling pipe-cleaner	oil pastels	glitter
craft glue	coloured pencils	sponge

2. Which part of the activity did you enjoy the most?

painting the background for the 'giant butterfly'

tracing the butterfly-shaped template

cutting out the traced template shape

using fanfolds to make the butterfly

fastening the folded butterfly with a pipe-cleaner

drawing the body for the butterfly

3. List three features of an insect.

_____   _____   _____

4. Use lead pencil to draw another insect. Colour your design using pencils. (Remember the features of an insect.)

R.I.C. Publications/Prim-Ed Publishing

Giant butterfly

Task assessment

Activity objectives

Arts ideas: *Creates artworks to express ideas.*

Arts skills and processes: *Uses a range of visual arts skills, techniques, procedures, practices and technologies.*

Arts responses: *Uses an aesthetic understanding to acknowledge, reflect on and assess the arts.*

Arts in society: *Demonstrates an understanding of the part that the arts play in society.*

Task

The students were instructed to make a 3-D 'giant butterfly' and background using a range of skills, techniques and materials.

Assessment key
✔ **yes** *(has demonstrated achievement of this criterion)*
✗ **no** *(has not demonstrated achievement of this criterion)*
● **inconsistent** *(some evidence of achievement has been shown)*

Criteria			
The student is able to:	✔	✗	●
participate in discussion about insects.			
demonstrate brush painting using paint.			
demonstrate sponging with 'pat and lift' technique.			
trace a cardboard template onto wrapping paper.			
cut out butterfly shape.			
demonstrate fan folding.			
twist a pipe-cleaner to fasten fanfolds.			
demonstrate drawing with strong, solid colour.			
complete a reflection sheet based on his/her artwork.			
listen to and follow instructions.			
work cooperatively in an informal activity-based work environment.			

Magnified fruit

This project was inspired by a lesson on 'healthy foods'. The children were asked to draw and colour healthy fruit.

Four-lesson project

Discussion points

An arrangement of fruit in a central location is the focus for the drawing; however, stimulus pictures of fruit will enhance meaningful discussion responses.

- What is your favourite fruit? (list fruit on the board)
- Why is fruit good for us? Discuss vitamins, minerals and fibre.
- Discuss the colours of different fruits.
- What is a magnifying glass? (A glass lens which, when looked through, enlarges what we can see.)

An arrangement of fruit in a central location, perhaps on the floor, with students positioned in a circle around it, works well.

Lesson one

Materials

- A4 photocopy paper
- fruit – real or pictures
- lead pencil/eraser
- permanent black marker
- newspaper to protect workspace

Method

1. Following discussion about fruit, the students use lead pencil to draw what they can see (pictures or real arrangement of fruit) onto A4 paper.
2. Trace over drawing with a thick permanent black marker.

Lesson two

Materials

- A4 drawing of the fruit
- A3 cartridge paper
- ★ black paper strips (2 strips 2 cm x 10 cm and 2 strips 2 cm x 12 cm)
- glue stick
- lead pencil
- permanent black marker
- newspaper to protect workspace

Method

1. Make a black frame by gluing the ends of the cardboard strips into a rectangle, as shown in example.
2. Move the frame around on the picture to locate a favourite part of it. This is called 'sectioning'.
3. Using lead pencil, draw the framed section onto A3 cartridge paper.
4. Trace with permanent black marker.

Lesson three

Materials

- A3 drawing of the fruit
- Edicol™ or vegetable dye
- paintbrushes (medium)
- wax crayons
- oil pastels
- coloured card to mount work
- craft glue for mounting

Method

1. Using wax crayons and oil pastels, colour the fruit. Oil pastels may be smudged to create a soft colour change, as shown in the example. Emphasise strong, solid colour.
2. Paint background using dye. Set aside to dry.
★ 3. Enlist adult to help to mount artwork.

Lesson four

Materials

- artwork in progress
- permanent black marker
- reflection and assessment photocopies
- lead pencil
- coloured pencils

Method

1. If necessary, darken lines by tracing over them with permanent black marker.
2. Students complete reflection activity.
3. Teacher completes assessment record.

R.I.C. Publications/Prim-Ed Publishing

Magnified fruit

R.I.C. Publications/Prim-Ed Publishing

Magnified fruit

Reflections

1. Circle the part of the activity you enjoyed the most.

drawing the fruit

tracing over the pencil lines with permanent black marker

making the cardboard frame to find sections

choosing a favourite section of the drawing

enlarging the chosen section of the drawing

colouring the fruit with wax crayons and oil pastels

painting around the fruit with dye

2. Were you pleased with your finished art piece?

Yes	No

Why?_____

_____

3. List five tools, materials and mediums you used to make your picture.

_____   _____   _____

_____   _____

4. (a) Draw a different fruit and section it with a drawn square.

   (b) Use lead pencil to draw the sectioned area.

(a)	(b)

Magnified fruit

Task assessment

Activity objectives

Arts ideas: *Creates artworks to express ideas.*

Arts skills and processes: *Uses a range of visual arts skills, techniques, procedures, practices and technologies.*

Arts responses: *Uses an aesthetic understanding to acknowledge, reflect on and assess the arts.*

Arts in society: *Demonstrates an understanding of the part that the arts play in society.*

Task

The students were instructed to make a 'magnified fruit' picture using a range of skills, techniques, mediums and materials.

Assessment key			
✔ **yes** (has demonstrated achievement of this criterion)			
✗ **no** (has not demonstrated achievement of this criterion)			
● **inconsistent** (some evidence of achievement has been shown)			
Criteria			
The student is able to:	✔	✗	●
participate in class discussion about fruit, colours of fruit and nutritional value.			
draw an arrangement of fruit using lead pencil.			
trace over drawing using permanent black marker.			
make a cardboard frame.			
use the cardboard frame to section a favourite part of his/her drawing.			
enlarge the sectioned part of their picture using lead pencil on A3 cartridge paper.			
trace over drawing using permanent black marker.			
demonstrate strong, solid colouring using wax crayons and oil pastels.			
paint background using dye.			
complete a reflection sheet based on his/her artwork.			
listen to and follow instructions.			
work cooperatively in an informal activity-based work environment.			

Parading penguins

This lesson is related to the environmental topic *Harsh environments*. The students were learning about the harsh regions of Antarctica and the Arctic Circle.

Two-lesson project

Discussion points

- What is a harsh environment? (extreme weather conditions)
- What animals survive in extremely cold, harsh environments? (polar bears, seals, penguins etc.)
- How do these animals survive? (fat insulation, feather insulation, migration to warmer areas during the most extreme cold conditions etc.)

Lesson one

Materials

- A3 cartridge paper
- acrylic paint
  - ~ blue for sky
  - ~ white
  - ~ yellow
  - ~ black
- sponges
- polystyrene paint trays
- paintbrush (medium)
- plastic food wrap
- ★ potato (medium size cut in half for each student)
- newspaper to protect workspace
- craft glue for mounting
- coloured card for mounting

Method

1. Following discussion about harsh environments and animal inhabitants, distribute A3 cartridge paper.
2. Using blue paint, students sponge paint entire page.
3. Spread out enough plastic food wrap to cover half the page when in portrait position.
4. Paint plastic wrap with white paint.
5. Press the painted side of plastic wrap onto the lower half of page. Carefully lift away and discard.
6. Use one half of the potato to print yellow paint for the sun.
7. Use remaining half of the potato to print black paint penguins. Three or four penguins are sufficient. (A penguin partially off page adds to illusion of realism.)
8. To print wings, press edge of potato in wing positions. Set aside to dry.
★ 9. Enlist adult to help to mount work onto coloured card before Lesson two.

Lesson two

Materials

- artwork in progress
- ★ potato (small size cut in half)
- acrylic paint
  - ~ white
  - ~ orange
- polystyrene trays (for paint)
- ★ polystyrene blocks cut into webbed foot and beak shapes
- craft knife (to cut polystyrene)
- permanent black marker
- newspaper to protect workspace
- reflection and assessment photocopies
- lead pencil
- coloured pencils

Method

1. Use potato to print white paint onto penguins to represent chest and stomach area.
2. Using polystyrene feet and beak shapes and orange paint, print feet and beaks.
3. Using flat end of pencil and white paint, print one white eye on each penguin. Set aside to dry.
4. Students complete reflection activity.
5. Teacher completes assessment record.
6. When dry, add eye detail using permanent black marker.

R.I.C. Publications/Prim-Ed Publishing

Parading penguins

R.I.C. Publications/Prim-Ed Publishing

Parading penguins

Reflections

1. Colour the mediums, materials and tools used to make your picture.

sponges	oil pastels	permanent black marker
blue paint	plastic food wrap	orange paint
black paint	black paper/card	potato
white paper/card	craft glue	polystyrene pieces
yellow paint	paintbrush	pencil

2. Circle the part of the activity you enjoyed the most.

sponge painting the background

printing the ice with white paint and plastic food wrap

using potatoes to print the penguins and the sun

printing the feet, beak and eye shapes

adding detail to the picture with permanent black marker

3. What is a 'harsh environment'?_____

_____

4. Name two animals which live in a harsh environment.

_____   _____

5. Use lead pencil to draw another animal which survives in a harsh environment. Colour the picture using pencils.

R.I.C. Publications/Prim-Ed Publishing

Parading penguins
Task assessment

Activity objectives
Arts ideas: *Creates artworks to express ideas.*
Arts skills and processes: *Uses a range of visual arts skills, techniques, procedures, practices and technologies.*
Arts responses: *Uses an aesthetic understanding to acknowledge, reflect on and assess the arts.*
Arts in society: *Demonstrates an understanding of the part that the arts play in society.*

Task
The students were instructed to make a penguin picture using
a range of skills, techniques, mediums and materials.

Assessment key			
✔ **yes** *(has demonstrated achievement of this criterion)*			
✗ **no** *(has not demonstrated achievement of this criterion)*			
● **inconsistent** *(some evidence of achievement has been shown)*			
Criteria			
The student is able to:	✔	✗	●
participate in class discussion about harsh environments and animal inhabitants.			
demonstrate sponge painting 'pat and lift' technique.			
paint plastic food wrap and press it onto a sponge painted surface.			
demonstrate printing with a potato, pencil end and polystyrene pieces.			
draw finishing detail with permanent black marker.			
complete a reflection sheet based on his/her artwork.			
listen to and follow instructions.			
work cooperatively in an informal activity-based work environment.			

Look who's looking through my window

This project may be related to any topic. The choices for the scene viewed from the window are limitless. The inspiration for this lesson was a trip to the zoo.

The students were told a fictitious story about a zoo animal visiting a young boy during the night and the adventure they had together. The students then wrote a similar narrative—which turns out to be a dream!

Two-lesson project

Discussion points

Following the storytelling, discuss the following:

- What was your favourite animal at the zoo? (List these on the board.)
- If you were allowed to keep this animal as a pet, where would you keep it? (List suggestions on board.)
- How would you feed your pet and with what? (List ideas on the board.)
- Where could you go with your zoo pet? (List places on the board.)
- Would you try to keep your pet a secret?
- Would you take your pet to school?
- What might happen at school?
- Is your pet able to stay with you or does it have to return to the zoo?
- All these questions prompt ideas for narrative writing preceding the art activity.
- Why do we keep animals in a zoo? (to allow people to see them without going into their natural habitat; to help save species by monitoring their breeding [making sure they don't become extinct])

Lesson one

Materials

- A4 photocopy paper
- A4 cartridge paper
- ★ photocopies of animal suggestions (pages 129–133)
- lead pencil
- permanent black marker
- paintbrushes (medium)
- wax crayons
- oil pastels
- Edicol™ or vegetable dye
- newspaper to protect workspace
- craft glue for mounting
- coloured card for mounting

Method

1. Using lead pencil, students draw the face of a zoo animal of their choice (see pages 129–133 for drawing suggestions) onto A4 photocopy paper.

2. When satisfied with their drawing, students use lead pencil to transfer their picture onto A4 cartridge paper.

3. Trace lines using permanent black marker.

4. Using wax crayons and oil pastels, colour animal and any background detail. Emphasise strong, solid colour.

5. Paint around coloured area using dye.

★ 6. Enlist adult help to mount pictures before Lesson two.

Lesson two

Materials

- artwork in progress
- ★ black card cut into strips
  4 strips 21 cm x 1.5 cm
  3 strips 29 cm x 1.5 cm
- glue stick
- newspaper to protect workspace
- reflection and assessment photocopies
- lead pencil
- coloured pencils

Method

1. Using glue stick, attach black card strips to picture to make the window frame (see example).

2. Students complete reflection activity.

3. Teacher completes assessment record.

Look who's looking through my window

Name: .... Date: ....

Look who's looking through my window

Reflections

1. Which animal did you choose for your picture? _____

2. What would your animal need to stay happy and healthy? _____

_____

3. Circle the part of the activity you enjoyed the most.

drawing the plan of your animal

transferring your drawing onto cartridge paper

tracing over your drawing with permanent black marker

colouring your picture with wax crayons and oil pastels

painting the background with dye

gluing the window frame onto your picture

4. Colour the mediums, materials and tools used to make your picture.

paint	sponges
glue stick	wax crayons
black card	scissors
paintbrush	dye
oil pastels	lead pencil
glitter	permanent black marker

5. Use lead pencil to draw another animal you would like to see through your window. Colour your picture with pencils.

100 *Primary art*

R.I.C. Publications/Prim-Ed Publishing

Look who's looking through my window

Task assessment

Activity objectives

Arts ideas: *Creates artworks to express ideas.*

Arts skills and processes: *Uses a range of visual arts skills, techniques, procedures, practices and technologies.*

Arts responses: *Uses an aesthetic understanding to acknowledge, reflect on and assess the arts.*

Arts in society: *Demonstrates an understanding of the part that the arts play in society.*

Task

The students were instructed to draw and frame their favourite zoo animal looking through their window, using a range of skills, techniques, mediums and materials.

Assessment key			
✔ **yes** (has demonstrated achievement of this criterion)			
✘ **no** (has not demonstrated achievement of this criterion)			
● **inconsistent** (some evidence of achievement has been shown)			
Criteria			
The student is able to:	✔	✘	●
listen to a fictitious story about a zoo animal visiting a young boy at home.			
participate in discussion about zoo animals.			
draw a plan of his/her favourite zoo animal.			
transfer the drawing to cartridge paper and trace over lead pencil lines with permanent black marker.			
demonstrate strong, solid colouring using wax crayons and oil pastels.			
paint background with dye.			
make a window frame using black card strips.			
complete a reflection sheet based on his/her artwork.			
listen to and follow instructions.			
work cooperatively in an informal activity-based work environment.			

Smudged colour explosion

This lesson was inspired by the theme *Colour*. Primary colours (red, yellow and blue) and the mixing of these to make secondary colours is demonstrated using the smudging technique. 'Special day' celebrations, including 'fireworks', were the focus of the 'colour explosions' created in this art piece.

Two-lesson project

Discussion points

- A colour wheel showing primary and secondary colours will stimulate meaningful discussion.
- What are the primary colours? (red, yellow and blue)
- Which primary colours blended together make orange? (yellow and red)
- Which colours blended together make purple? (red and blue)
- Which colours blended together make green? (yellow and blue)
- On what occasions do we celebrate and use bright colours to enhance the celebration? (parties—balloons, streamers; events where fireworks are a focus—to celebrate New Year, a national day, the beginning or conclusion of an event etc.)
- Have you been to an event where fireworks were part of the entertainment/celebration? (List responses on the board.) Discuss how fireworks explode into colour.

Lesson one

Materials

- A3 cartridge paper
- oil pastels
- newspaper to protect workspace
- coloured card for mounting
- craft glue for mounting

Method

1. Following discussion about colour, fireworks and celebrations, the students use primary colour oil pastels to draw five small circles to represent the centre of firework explosions. In a rosette formation, with back and forth movements, draw circles around centre dot until rosettes almost meet. If there is a gap/blank spot on the page, draw half a rosette.

2. Using index finger, gently drag colour from the centre of circles, outwards. (Ensure finger is clean when commencing different colour rosettes.)

★ 3. Enlist adult help to mount work.

Lesson two

Materials

- reflection and assessment photocopies
- lead pencil
- coloured pencils

Method

1. Students complete reflection activity.

2. Teacher completes assessment record.

Smudged colour explosion

Reflections

1. *Circle the part of the activity you enjoyed more.*

    drawing the oil pastel rosettes using a back and forth motion

    smudging the primary colour rosettes to make 'firework explosions'

2. *Why did you enjoy this part of the activity more?*

    _____

    _____

3. *Which two primary colours blended together make ...*

    (a) orange? _____   _____

    (b) green? _____   _____

    (c) purple? _____   _____

4. List two celebration activities which include fireworks to entertain us.

    _____   _____

5. *Why do you enjoy watching a fireworks display?*

    _____

    _____

6. *Draw yourself at a celebration event. Colour your picture using secondary and primary colours.*

    ┌───┐
    │   │
    │   │
    │   │
    │   │
    │   │
    │   │
    │   │
    │   │
    │   │
    └───┘

R.I.C. Publications/Prim-Ed Publishing

Smudged colour explosion
Task assessment

Activity objectives

Arts ideas: *Creates artworks to express ideas.*

Arts skills and processes: *Uses a range of visual arts skills, techniques, procedures, practices and technologies.*

Arts responses: *Uses an aesthetic understanding to acknowledge, reflect on and assess the arts.*

Arts in society: *Demonstrates an understanding of the part that the arts play in society.*

Task

The students were instructed to make a 'smudged colour' representation of a fireworks display using a range of skills, techniques, mediums and materials.

Assessment key			
✔ **yes** *(has demonstrated achievement of this criterion)*			
✗ **no** *(has not demonstrated achievement of this criterion)*			
● **inconsistent** *(some evidence of achievement has been shown)*			
Criteria			
The student is able to:	✔	✗	●
participate in discussion about primary colours, celebrations and fireworks.			
use oil pastel and primary colours to draw rosettes with a back and forth motion.			
demonstrate strong, solid colouring while drawing rosettes.			
smudge rosettes from the centre outwards.			
complete a reflection sheet based on his/her artwork.			
listen to and follow instructions.			
work cooperatively in an informal activity-based work environment.			

Busy town

This lesson relates to several areas; maths, mapping, places in our environment, health (safety on the roads), rules and road signs, and language (writing a narrative about an adventure in the town or city and brainstorming words to enrich vocabulary).

Three-lesson project

Discussion points

- What things are in the environment in which we live? Brainstorm and list responses on the board. (houses, roads, cars, school, playground, shops etc.)
- Draw a stop sign. What does this sign mean? (stop at the white line)
- What other signs have you noticed when you are walking or travelling in a car? (give way, traffic lights, school, speed limit signs etc.)
- What sorts of vehicles do you see travelling on the road? (trucks, cars, motorcycles, bikes, buses, vans, caravans and trailers etc.)
- Apart from stop signs, what else can warn us to slow down, stop or go? (traffic lights: amber—slow down, red—stop, green—go.)
- Each student can create his/her street and surrounding streets, ensuring it is a busy time of day by including traffic.

Lesson one

Materials

- A4 photocopy paper
- A3 cartridge paper
- coloured paper squares
- ★ silver metallic paper (cut into strips 1.5 cm wide)
- dot stickers (2 sizes)
- ★ scrap white paper (cut into strips 1 cm wide)
- ★ black paper/card (cut into strips 6 cm wide)
- wax crayons
- green paint
- blue paint
- polystyrene trays (for paint)
- scrap cereal box card (small pieces to use the edges for printing grass)
- ★ sponges (cut into small blocks)
- lead pencil
- ruler
- permanent black marker
- glue stick
- newspaper to protect workspace
- scissors

Method

1. Following discussion about the environment, towns/cities, road signs and rules, students use lead pencil to draw a plan of a 'busy town' scene onto A4 paper.
2. Using lead pencil, transfer plan onto A3 paper.
3. Using black card strips, position roads onto A3 cartridge paper. Cut to size with scissors.

4. Using glue stick, glue roads into position.
5. Cut white paper strips into short lengths and glue white lines onto roads. (Include 'stop' lines at intersections.)
6. Using wax crayons, draw any detail appropriate to plan—in the example, the playground equipment. Emphasise strong, solid colour.
7. Using lead pencil, rule rectangles, triangles and squares onto the back of coloured paper to make buildings.
8. Cut out shapes.
9. Position and glue buildings into place using glue stick.
10. Cut silver metallic paper into short lengths to make windows. Position windows and glue into place using glue stick.
11. Using lead pencil, draw shapes to make vehicles and road signs onto the back of coloured paper and cut them out.
12. Position on page and glue into place using glue stick.
13. Use circle/dot stickers for wheels.
14. Using permanent black marker, add detail to picture.
15. Using small sponges and blue and green paint, sponge background. Emphasise 'pat and lift' technique.
16. Using the edge of cereal card and green paint, print grass detail. Set aside to dry.

Lesson two

Materials

- artwork in progress
- materials for Lesson one
- card for mounting
- craft glue for mounting

Method

1. Students complete 'busy town' picture.
★ 2. Enlist adult help to mount picture onto coloured card.

Lesson three

Materials

- reflection and assessment photocopies
- lead pencil
- coloured pencils

Method

1. Students complete reflection activity.
2. Teacher completes assessment record.

R.I.C. Publications/Prim-Ed Publishing

Busy town

R.I.C. Publications/Prim-Ed Publishing

Busy town

Reflections

1. List four things you are likely to find in a busy town.

   _____   _____

   _____   _____

2. Circle the part of the activity you enjoyed most.

   drawing the plan for your 'busy town' picture and transferring it to the large paper

   drawing and colouring features onto your picture using wax crayons

   drawing and cutting out the paper shapes to make your 'busy town' picture

   gluing the paper shapes onto your picture

   adding detail to your picture using permanent black marker

   sponge painting to colour background

   printing grass with the edge of card

3. Why did you like this part of the activity the most?

   _____

   _____

4. Traffic lights help to stop accidents from happening.
   Explain what each light means.

   amber _____

   red _____

   green _____

5. Use a lead pencil to draw your favourite part of your picture.
   Colour your drawing with pencils.

R.I.C. Publications/Prim-Ed Publishing

Busy town

Task assessment

Activity objectives

Arts ideas: *Creates artworks to express ideas.*

Arts skills and processes: *Uses a range of visual arts skills, techniques, procedures, practices and technologies.*

Arts responses: *Uses an aesthetic understanding to acknowledge, reflect on and assess the arts.*

Arts in society: *Demonstrates an understanding of the part that the arts play in society.*

Task

The students were instructed to make a 'busy town' picture using a range of skills, techniques, mediums and materials.

Assessment key			
✔ **yes** *(has demonstrated achievement of this criterion)*			
✗ **no** *(has not demonstrated achievement of this criterion)*			
● **inconsistent** *(some evidence of achievement has been shown)*			
Criteria			
The student is able to:	✔	✗	●
participate in class discussion about towns, road signs and road safety rules.			
draw and transfer a plan of a 'busy town' using lead pencil.			
position paper/card road strips and glue them into place.			
cut white paper strips for road lines and glue them into place.			
demonstrate drawing and colouring with strong, solid colour using wax crayons.			
use lead pencil to rule rectangles, squares and other shapes onto the back of coloured paper to make buildings and vehicles.			
cut out shapes using scissors.			
cut metallic strips into small rectangles to make windows.			
position and glue picture pieces into position.			
add detail using permanent black marker.			
sponge paint using a 'pat and lift' technique.			
print grass using the edge of cereal box card and acrylic paint.			
complete a reflection sheet based on his/her artwork.			
listen to and follow instructions.			
work cooperatively in an informal activity-based work environment.			

All shapes and sizes collage

This lesson was inspired by the maths topic *Shape and space*. The focus was on basic 2-D shapes and the characteristics of each.

Two-lesson project

Discussion points

This lesson is a part of a series of maths lessons on shapes and is a creative way of reinforcing concepts. Large cardboard shapes are a useful teaching tool.

- What is a square?
- What is a rectangle?
- What is a circle?
- What is a triangle?
  (Discuss the characteristics of each.)

Lesson one

Materials

- A4 cartridge paper
- ★ prepared shape templates (page 134)
- permanent black marker
- wax crayons and/or oil pastels
- Edicol™ or vegetable dye
- paintbrush (medium)
- craft glue (for mounting and enhancing work with glitter- optional)
- glitter (various colours) (optional)
- polystyrene trays (for craft glue)
- paintbrush (fine)
- coloured card for mounting
- newspaper to protect workspace

Method

1. Following discussion of shapes and their characteristics, students use permanent black marker to trace prepared templates onto A4 cartridge paper (approximately two of each shape).

2. Colour sections using wax crayons or oil pastels. Emphasise strong, solid colour.

3. Leave three small sections blank to include glitter enhancement (optional).

4. Paint around coloured shapes using dye.

★ 5. Enlist adult help to assist children to paint craft glue onto blank spaces and sprinkle with glitter (optional).

★ 6. Enlist adult help to mount work onto coloured card.

Lesson two

Materials

- reflection and assessment photocopies
- lead pencil
- coloured pencils

Method

1. Students complete reflection activity.

2. Teacher completes assessment record.

R.I.C. Publications/Prim-Ed Publishing

All shapes and sizes collage

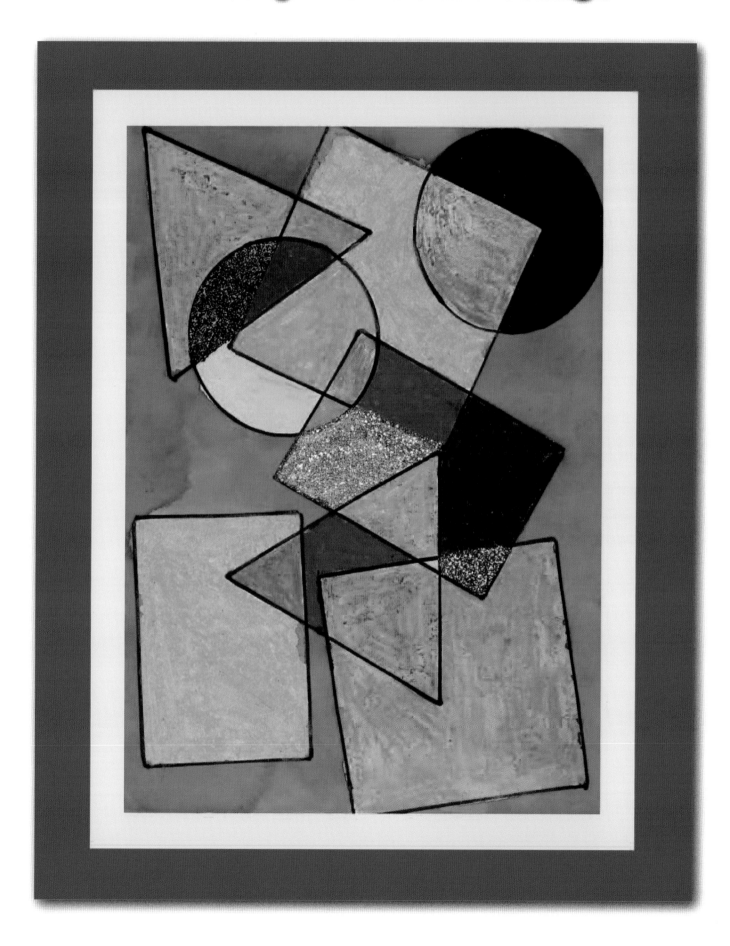

R.I.C. Publications/Prim-Ed Publishing

All shapes and sizes collage

Reflections

1. Colour the mediums, materials and tools used to make your collage.

wax crayons	craft glue	coloured paper
scissors	cartridge paper	dye
shape templates	paintbrushes	lead pencil
glue stick	glitter	oil pastels

2. Circle the part of the activity you enjoyed the most.

tracing the shape templates onto the cartridge paper

colouring the shapes

painting the dye around the shapes

enhancing work with glitter

3. List the number of sides the following shapes have.

triangle _____   **circle** _____

square _____   **rectangle** _____

4. Use a lead pencil to draw a square, rectangle, triangle and circle.
   Colour the shapes with pencils.

R.I.C. Publications/Prim-Ed Publishing

All shapes and sizes collage
Task assessment

Activity objectives

Arts ideas: *Creates artworks to express ideas.*

Arts skills and processes: *Uses a range of visual arts skills, techniques, procedures, practices and technologies.*

Arts responses: *Uses an aesthetic understanding to acknowledge, reflect on and assess the arts.*

Arts in society: *Demonstrates an understanding of the part that the arts play in society.*

Task

The students were instructed to make a 'shape collage' using a range of skills, techniques and materials.

Assessment key			
✔ **yes** *(has demonstrated achievement of this criterion)*			
✗ **no** *(has not demonstrated achievement of this criterion)*			
● **inconsistent** *(some evidence of achievement has been shown)*			
Criteria			
The student is able to:	✔	✗	●
participate in class discussion about shapes.			
trace shape template onto cartridge paper using permanent black marker.			
colour traced shapes using wax crayons and/or oil pastels and strong, solid colour.			
paint dye around the coloured shapes.			
complete a reflection sheet based on his/her artwork.			
listen to and follow instructions.			
work cooperatively in an informal activity-based work environment.			

Rainbow iceblocks on sticks

This project was inspired by the theme *Summer*.

Three-lesson project

Discussion points

- What are the four seasons? (summer, autumn, winter, spring)
- In which season do we most enjoy having cold treats? (summer—when the weather is warmer.)
- What is your favourite cold summer treat? (icy poles, ice-cream, chilled fruit etc.)
- Why is an ice-cream a treat and not a healthy food? (lots of sugar; emphasise that ice-creams are a treat and we should only eat them occasionally)
- What are the primary colours? (red, blue, yellow) If desired, revise colour mixing of primary colours. Red and blue make purple, blue and yellow make green, yellow and red make orange.

Lesson one

Materials

- A3 cartridge paper (2 sheets per child)
- wax crayons
- Edicol™ or vegetable dye (primary colours)
- paintbrushes (medium)
- newspaper to protect workspace
- coloured card for mounting background
- craft glue for mounting

Method

1. Following discussion, with A3 cartridge paper in landscape position, demonstrate painting with dye, using the three primary colours. Paint very wet horizontal stripes. Commence with yellow, then red, then blue. Hold work vertically to allow colours to run together in a rainbow of colour.
2. Students complete the process to make their own artwork. Set aside to dry.
3. Locate a rough, textured surface.
4. Using wax crayon, rub crayon over second sheet of A3 cartridge paper while leaning on rough surface to create a texture rubbing.
5. Using a contrasting primary colour, paint with dye over texture rubbing. Set aside to dry.
6. Enlist adult help to mount texture rubbing background onto coloured card before Lesson two.

Lesson two

Materials

- artwork in progress
- prepared iceblock shape template (page 135)
- cereal box cardboard
- craft sticks
- craft glue
- newspaper to protect workspace
- scissors
- glue stick
- permanent black marker

Method

1. Using glue stick generously, glue rainbow coloured paper onto cereal box cardboard.
2. Using prepared template and permanent black marker, trace four iceblock shapes onto the cereal box cardboard.
3. Cut out shapes and attach craft sticks, using craft glue, to the back of iceblock shapes. Set aside to dry.

Lesson three

Materials

- artwork in progress
- craft glue (squeeze bottle)
- lead pencil
- coloured pencils
- reflection and assessment photocopies

Method

1. Arrange iceblocks on background.
2. Using craft glue, attach iceblocks to background.
3. Students complete reflection activity.
4. Teacher completes assessment record.

R.I.C. Publications/Prim-Ed Publishing

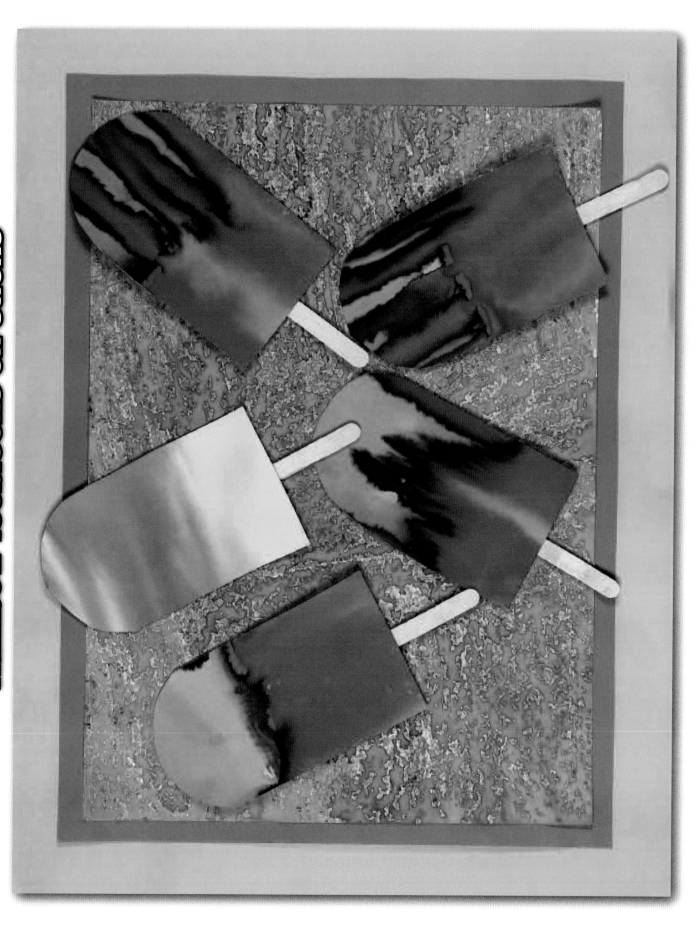

Rainbow iceblocks on sticks

R.I.C. Publications/Prim-Ed Publishing

Rainbow iceblocks on sticks

Reflections

1. *Colour the mediums and materials used to make your collage.*

wax crayons	oil pastels	dye
craft sticks	craft glue	glitter
paint	iceblock template	metallic paper

2. *Circle the part of the activity you enjoyed the most.*

painting a rainbow sheet with dye

making a texture rubbing and dye background

tracing the iceblock shape template

cutting out the iceblock shapes

gluing the sticks onto the iceblock shapes

arranging the iceblocks onto the background

gluing the rainbow iceblocks into position

3. *Why should we eat ice-cream and icy poles only as a treat?*

_____

_____

_____

_____

_____

_____

4. *What are the three primary colours?*

_____

_____

5. *Draw a rainbow ice-cream using yellow and blue to make the rainbow colour.*

R.I.C. Publications/Prim-Ed Publishing

Rainbow iceblocks on sticks
Task assessment

Activity objectives

Arts ideas: *Creates artworks to express ideas.*

Arts skills and processes: *Uses a range of visual arts skills, techniques, procedures, practices and technologies.*

Arts responses: *Uses an aesthetic understanding to acknowledge, reflect on and assess the arts.*

Arts in society: *Demonstrates an understanding of the part that the arts play in society.*

Task

The students were instructed to make a collage of iceblocks on sticks using
a range of skills, techniques, mediums and materials.

Assessment key			
✔ **yes** *(has demonstrated achievement of this criterion)*			
✗ **no** *(has not demonstrated achievement of this criterion)*			
● **inconsistent** *(some evidence of achievement has been shown)*			
Criteria			
The student is able to:	✔	✗	●
participate in class discussion about summer, summer treats and primary colours.			
paint using dye to create a rainbow of colours.			
make a texture rubbing using wax crayon.			
painting dye over texture rubbing.			
glue rainbow paper onto cereal box card using glue stick.			
trace an iceblock shape template.			
cut out traced iceblock shapes.			
glue sticks onto iceblock shapes.			
arrange iceblocks in a collage on texture rubbing background.			
glue iceblocks into position.			
complete a reflection sheet based on his/her artwork.			
listen to and follow instructions.			
work cooperatively in an informal activity-based work environment.			

Busy bee

This lesson was inspired by the theme *Insects*. Stimulus photos of insects will enhance discussion.

Three-lesson project

Discussion points ○○○

- What is an insect? (a small invertebrate with 3 body parts, 3 pairs of legs and usually 2 pairs of wings)
- What insects do you know? (bee, grasshopper, cricket, mosquito, butterfly etc.)
- Where have you seen a bee? (Most answers will relate to gardens.)
- What do bees make that we enjoy eating? (honey)
- What do bees have which can hurt us? (a sting)
- What sound do bees make? (a soft hum, buzz)
- What do bees do that helps flowers? (They spread the pollen from one flower to another, which enables the flowers to become pollinated and produce seeds.)

Lesson one ○○

Materials

- A3 cartridge paper
- oil pastels/wax crayons
- 2 small uncoated paper plates
- acrylic paint (blue, green and colours suitable for a flower centre and petals)
- polystyrene trays (for paint)
- sponges
- lead pencil
- craft glue for mounting
- coloured card for mounting
- newspaper to protect workspace

Method

1. Following discussion about bees, students use wax crayons or oil pastels to draw a large stem and leaves on A3 cartridge paper. Emphasise strong, solid colour.
2. Use sponges to paint right sides of paper plates. On one plate, sponge the edge a different colour from the centre to make the centre and petals of the flower distinct.
3. Sponge paint the leaves green and background blue using a 'pat and lift' technique. Set aside to dry.
★ 4. Enlist adult to help mount background before Lesson two.

Lesson two ○○

Materials

- artwork in progress
★ - prepared flower and wing-templates (page 136)
★ - yellow and black card cut into strips 6 cm x 42 cm
- large and small plain coloured sticker circles (for eyes) (If 22 mm metallic stickers are available, these look effective as an eye background.)
- sparkling pipe-cleaners (3 halves for legs) (1 half for antennae)
- metallic crepe paper for wings
- glue stick
- scissors
- hot glue gun
- craft glue (squeeze bottle)
- stapler
- permanent black marker
- newspaper to protect workspace

Method

1. Trace flower template onto the back of both paper plates.
2. Cut along traced lines.
3. Using craft glue, attach top plate to bottom plate to form flower. Glue flower onto background at the top of the stem.
4. Staple together ends of black and yellow strips at right angles (see below) and paper fold. Make sure at least one end finishes with a yellow fold. Secure ends together.

5. Make eyes by pressing stickers in position.
6. Draw eye detail with permanent black marker.
★ 7. Bend four pipe-cleaners in half, and, with adult assistance, hot glue into place.
8. Turn feet and antennae ends outwards.
9. Trace wing template onto the back of metallic crepe paper.
10. Cut out circles and, using glue stick, attach to middle fold.
11. Using scissors, cut across middle of bee's face from point to point to form a triangle.
12. Glue yellow section of face to black section.
13. Using craft glue, attach bee to background.

Lesson three ○○○

Materials

- artwork in progress
- craft glue
- paintbrush (fine)
- polystyrene tray (for craft glue)
- glitter (green, gold and silver) (optional)
- reflection and assessment photocopies
- lead pencil
- coloured pencils

Method

1. Using fine paintbrush and craft glue, paint area requiring glitter enhancement.
★ 2. Sprinkle with glitter.
3. Students complete reflection activity.
4. Teacher completes assessment record.

Busy bee

Busy bee

Reflections

1. Colour the materials, mediums and tools used to make your picture.

cartridge paper	permanent black marker	paper plates	lead pencil
paint	wax crayons	dye	paintbrush
sponges	craft glue	glitter	tissue paper
glue stick	sparkling pipe-cleaners	oil pastels	baking paper

2. Circle the part of the activity you enjoyed the most.

drawing the stem and leaves with strong, solid colour

sponge painting the background, leaves and paper plates

tracing the flower template onto the back of paper plates

cutting out the flowers

folding the card strips to make the bee

making the pipe-cleaner legs and antennae for the bee

making the wings by tracing the circle, cutting them out and gluing them onto the body

adding the eyes

adding glitter to enhance your picture

3. Circle the features of an insect.

six body parts

three body parts

eight legs

six legs

an outside skeleton

usually has wings

six pairs of wings

nine antennae

4. Use lead pencil to draw another insect. Colour your design using pencils. (Remember the features of an insect.)

Busy bee
Task assessment

Activity objectives

Arts ideas: *Creates artworks to express ideas.*

Arts skills and processes: *Uses a range of visual arts skills, techniques, procedures, practices and technologies.*

Arts responses: *Uses an aesthetic understanding to acknowledge, reflect on and assess the arts.*

Arts in society: *Demonstrates an understanding of the part that the arts play in society.*

Task

The students were instructed to make a paper fold 'busy bee' and background using a range of skills, techniques and materials.

Assessment key		
✔ **yes** (has demonstrated achievement of this criterion)		
✗ **no** (has not demonstrated achievement of this criterion)		
● **inconsistent** (some evidence of achievement has been shown)		
Criteria		
The student is able to:	✔	✗	●
participate in discussion about insects.			
demonstrate strong, solid colour using wax crayons and/or oil pastels.			
sponge paint using 'pat and lift' technique.			
trace a prepared template using lead pencil.			
cut out traced shapes.			
fold paper strips in a crisscross format as demonstrated.			
trace a prepared circle template for wings.			
cut out traced circles.			
glue wing circles into position.			
glue completed bee into position on background.			
add glitter enhancement to picture.			
complete a reflection sheet based on his/her artwork.			
listen to and follow instructions.			
work cooperatively in an informal activity-based work environment.			

Resources

Templates should be made from card, such as cereal box/lightweight strawboard. Adults can help to make templates prior to lessons, depending on the age and ability of students and the difficulty of the art project. Instructions for some templates are given, although teachers may design their own or alter sizes to suit.

Be environmentally friendly by using household packaging to make sets of reusable templates.

Spring is in the air

Enlarge to appropriate size.

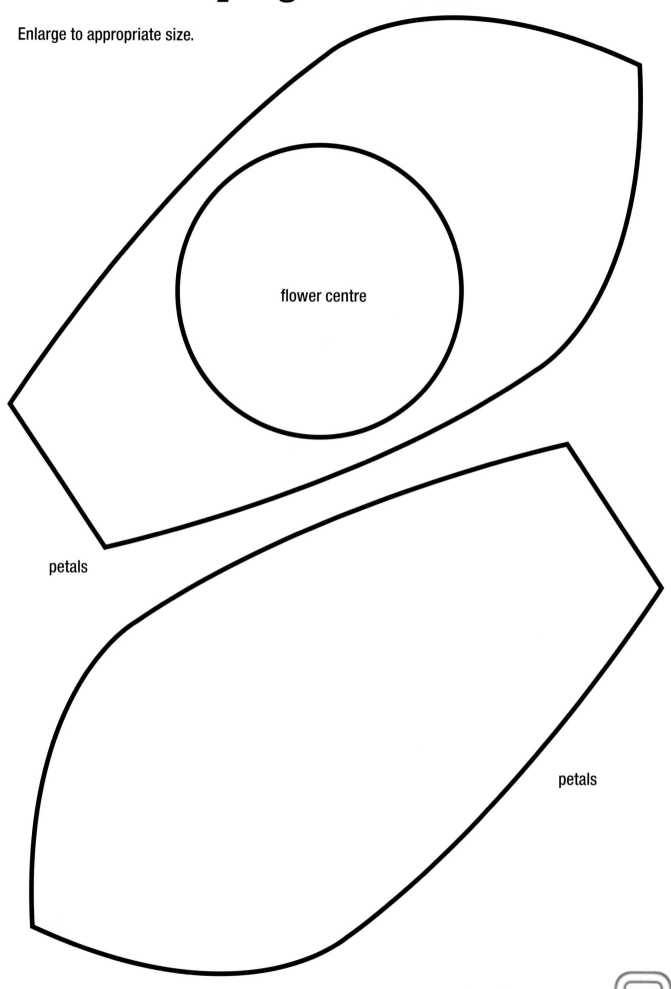

flower centre

petals

petals

R.I.C. Publications/Prim-Ed Publishing

Fancy fish plaques

R.I.C. Publications/Prim-Ed Publishing

Leaping lizards

Enlarge to appropriate size.

R.I.C. Publications/Prim-Ed Publishing

Autumn leaves repetitive drawing collage

Rock and roll tie

Enlarge to appropriate size.

R.I.C. Publications/Prim-Ed Publishing

Birds of peacefulness

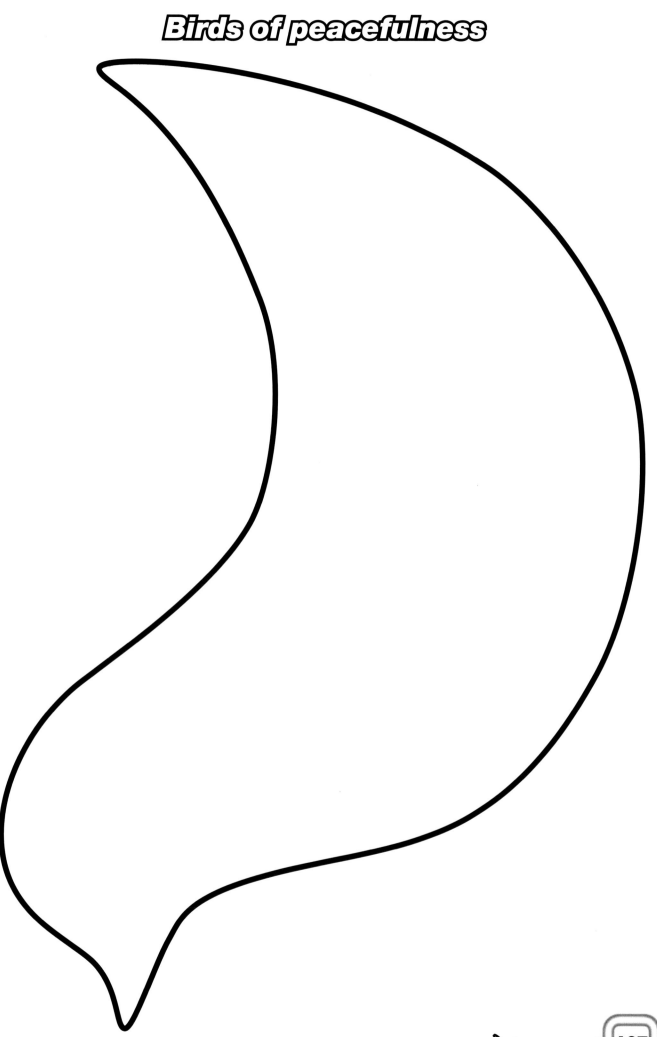

R.I.C. Publications/Prim-Ed Publishing

Giant butterfly

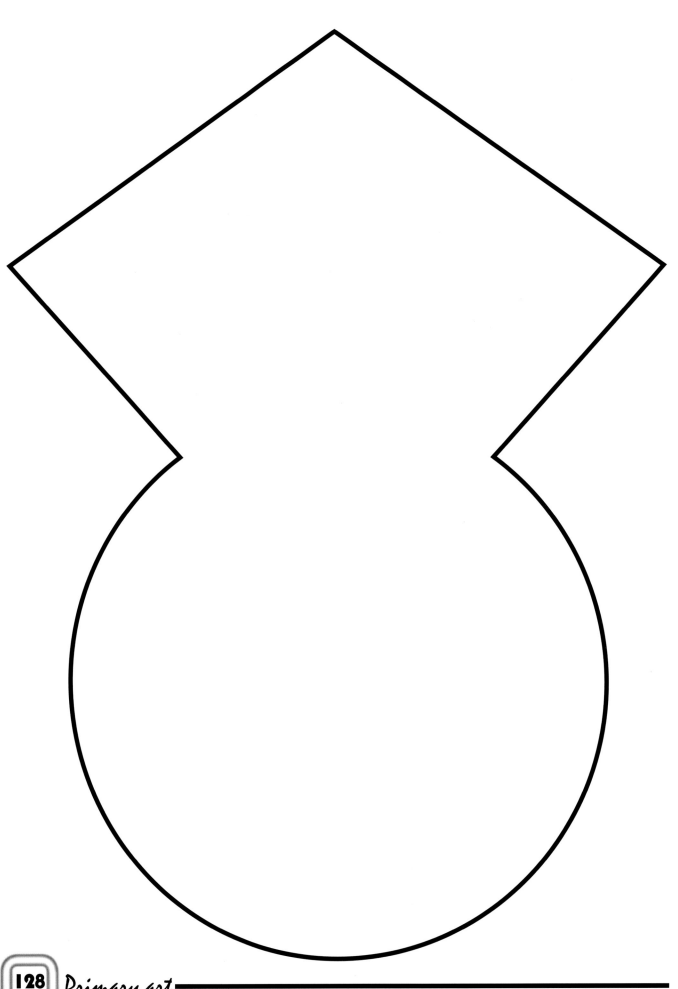

R.I.C. Publications/Prim-Ed Publishing

Look who's looking through my window

Enlarge to appropriate size.

Look who's looking through my window

Enlarge to appropriate size.

R.I.C. Publications/Prim-Ed Publishing

Look who's looking through my window

Enlarge to appropriate size.

Look who's looking through my window

Enlarge to appropriate size.

R.I.C. Publications/Prim-Ed Publishing

Look who's looking through my window

Enlarge to appropriate size.

All shapes and sizes collage

Enlarge to appropriate size.

R.I.C. Publications/Prim-Ed Publishing

Rainbow iceblocks on sticks

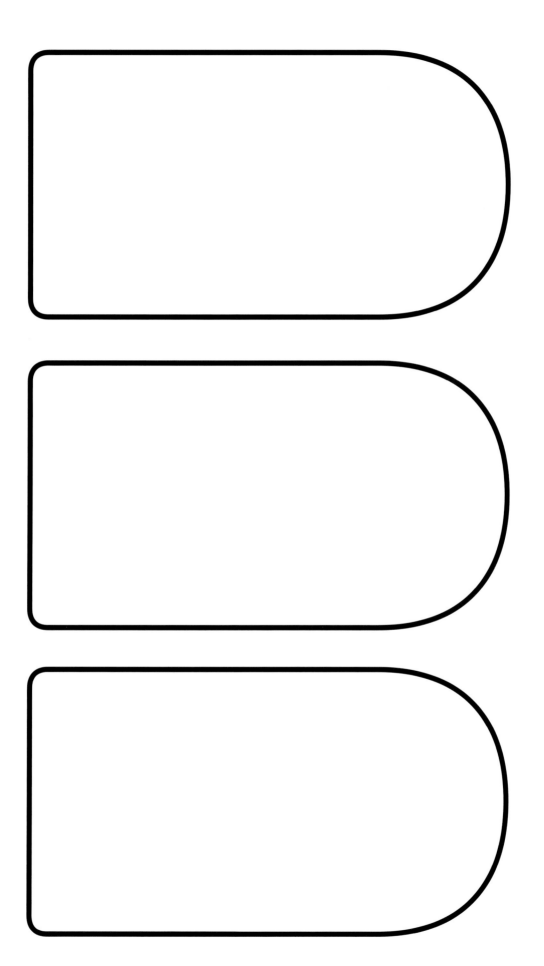

Busy bee

Enlarge to paper plate size.

Wing circles

R.I.C. Publications/Prim-Ed Publishing